A Season on the Appalachian Trail

A season on the
Appalachian Trail

an american odyssey

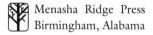 Lynn Setzer

Menasha Ridge Press
Birmingham, Alabama

Library of Congress Cataloging-in-Publication Data

Setzer, Lynn, 1955–
A Season on the Appalachian Trail: An American Odyssey / by Lynn Setzer.
    p. cm.
    ISBN 0-89732-234-7
  1. Hiking—Appalachian Trail. 2. Appalachian Trail—Anecdotes.
  3. Appalachian Trail—Description and Travel.   I. Title.
GV199.42.A68S48   1997
796.51'0974—dc21   97-9758
                                                              CIP

Cover design by Grant Tatum
Cover photograph by Grant Tatum
Back cover photograph by Lynn Setzer
Text design by Kandace Hawkinson
Inside photographs by Lynn Setzer, copyright © 1997
(except for page 177, provided by Wildhair)
Cartography by Sue Irwin

Selection from "After a While" reprinted here
with permission of Veronica A. Shoffstall, © 1971.
Edward Abbey quote reprinted here with
permission of EarthFirst!

Menasha Ridge Press
700 South 28th Street, Suite 206
Birmingham, AL 35233
(800) 247-9437

To Randall and Sumo,
who both cut me some slack.

c o n t e n t s

a c k n o w l e d g e m e n t s

Sooner or later thru-hikers learn that a little help, either that which they give or that which they receive, is a wonderful thing. The same goes for a writer writing about thru-hikers. The people to whom I am indebted include:

- Several members of the Trail community: the Amicalola Park Rangers, Jeff and Dorothy Hansen and their able staff at the Walasi-Yi Center, Mark Wiggins and Mark O'Connor of the Nantahala Outdoor Center, Gina Sessons of the Great Smoky Mountain Diner, "Damascus Dave" Patrick of Mount Rogers Outfitters and '90 thru-hiker, Elizabeth McKee, mayor of Damascus, Virginia, Paul Lethcoe, caretaker of The Place in Damascus, and Laurie Potteiger and Brian King of the Appalachian Trail Conference, Father Fred Alvarez of Graymoor Friary, Steve Longley of The Forks, Maine, and Keith Shaw of Monson, Maine.

- A pocketful of former thru-hikers: Squirrel '94, and the 1996 GATC ridgerunner, Bad DNA '94, Jester '94, Neill Ross '73, Bald Eagle '92, Tarkus '92, Zontian Granny '95, Full Moon and Celestial Spirit '95, and Lancer (do not recall when he thru-hiked). Sparkler '91 and '92: thanks for the postcard! I was very glad to get the '96 AT Trail Days postmark.

■ All of the class of '96 who talked with me, but especially Marmot and Allgood for your vote of confidence, and Craigmont, for the darn fine beer you treated me to in Port Clinton, Pennsylvania. (That was a hot day and a cold beer; it couldn't have been a better match.) Bloody Nose and Wildhair: thanks for the pictures of your summit. (Sorry I couldn't have been there on those days!) Nomad, Lea, and Ranger Dave: thanks for the special postcards you sent me. Kick-a-Tree and Trail Gimp: to you goes a special acknowledgment for having the courage to share your stories of a thru-hike that didn't quite make it. You probably speak for more hikers than you'll ever know.

■ Lee Shapiro of the Morehead Planetarium, University of North Carolina, Chapel Hill, for astronomical assistance.

■ The good folks back at the ranches I occasionally haunt: Jim Setzer, Edward Renfrow, Gwen Canady, Curtis Clark, Dennis McCarty, Gregg Kreizman, the Five Angry Women, Becky in Seattle, and, of course, Mom and Dad.

I am not a thru-hiker. This is not something that one can pretend to be and get away with it. However, hiking on the Appalachian Trail is one of my favorite pastimes, and writing this book is partially an outgrowth of that. Lucky me that I was able to add to my accumulation of miles!

In researching and writing this book, I decided that my primary rule would be to impact the thru-hikers' hikes only as much as I would need to capture and tell a legitimate story. They did not decide to hike so that I could write a book; rather, as they hiked, they were gracious enough to share their experiences and stories with me, different hikers at different times. My second rule was that I would collect their stories and observations either as they happened or very soon afterward. I did not want the romance of time to substantively change their stories. My third rule was, so far as possible, they would tell their stories in their own words. They did, after all, do the hiking.

I used several methods to meet hikers and collect their stories and comments. The first was to meet them face to face. I hiked portions of the Trail, introduced myself when I found a thru-hiker and asked if he or she would like to share their experiences. I walked in the woods with my notepad quite often: on the Springer Mountain Approach Trail and on Blood Mountain, Georgia; near Wallace Gap, Wayah Bald, Tellico Gap, the Smokies, and on Max Patch in North Carolina; in and around Mount

Rogers, Grayson Highlands, throughout Shenandoah in Virginia; across Weverton Cliffs in Maryland; in Pine Grove Furnace State Park, in St. Anthony's Wilderness, and the Delaware Water Gap, in Pennsylvania; near Oil City Road in New Jersey; over Bear Mountain and through the Trailside Zoo in New York; above treeline in the White Mountains and near Pinkham Notch in New Hampshire; in the Bigelow Nature Preserve, Abol Bridge, and through Baxter State Park in Maine. Occasionally I stationed myself where the Appalachian Trail exits the woods and waited for hikers to appear so that I could strike up a conversation. These places included Stecoah Gap and Fontana Dam, North Carolina; Clingman's Dome and Newfound Gap, Tennessee; Harper's Ferry, West Virginia; Gathland State Park, Maryland; Port Clinton and Hawk Mountain, Pennsylvania; Hessian Lake, New York; and several Maine logging roads. Sometimes I visited the hostels and other places where thru-hikers bunk and stayed with them when there was room: Neels Gap, Georgia; Nantahala Outdoor Center and the Jesuit Hostel in Hot Springs, North Carolina; The Place in Damascus and the Visitor's Center at Mt. Rogers, Virginia; Ironmaster's Hostel at Boiling Springs and the Doyle Hotel in Duncannon; Graymoor Friary, New York; Mt. Greylock Lodge, Massachusetts; Zealand Falls hut and Mt. Madison hut, White Mountains, New Hampshire; and Shaw's Boarding House, Maine.

Hikers I met in these ways include 007, Ajax, Allgood, Annapurna, Attitude, Bear, Beorn, Big Jim, Blister Free, Bloody Nose, Bojangles, Bonnie and Clyde, Breakin' Wind, Buc-Buc, Bull Moose, Bungalow Bill and Contrary Mary, Buzz, Cajun C and Screamin Knees, Calvin and Hobbes, Captain Chucky, Caspar, Catfish, the Cat in the Hat and Blueberry, Chomp Cat, Cold Finger, Cornhusker, Cough Drop, Cowardly Lion, Craigmont, CrossStone, Cub, Damn Near Bootless, Doc, Drooling Dear, Early Mon, FAS, Firefly, the Fru, Gearmaster, Gizzie, Golden Eagle, the Golden Kiwis, Gray Rabbit, Greyhound, Greywolf, Guildenstern, Gumby, Gwic, H, Hans Solo, the Hiking Vikings, Heavy Breather, Home Brew, Jabberwocky, Jarhead and Loon Lady, Jester, Johnny Quest (the northbounder), Julie McCoy Cruise Director, Kick-a-Tree, K-Posa, Kiwi, Lady Bug, Lazy Bones, Lemstar, Little Bear, Lobo's pet, Lone Wolf, Lord Bacon, Mailman, M&M, Marmot, Medicine Woman, Midnight, Mr. Bean, Mr. and Mrs. Honeymooner, Mr. Maine, Morning Glory, Mover and Mosey, Munchkin, Navigator (the nice one), Nomad, No Trail Name, Oak, Obe-1-Knobe, Out of Africa, Paw Paw, Pilgrim, Pirate, Plimsoul, Pokey, Pony Express, Poohbear, Q-Tip, Quid Pro Quo, Rafiki,

Robohiker, Rogue Bear, Rumpel, Runaway Ralph, Sandman, Scamper and Rosey, Scout, Seadog, Silver Fox, Sisyphus the Happy, Skylark, Sluggo, Spare, Squirrel, Strider, Stringbean, SunSpirit, Sven, Sweet Dreams, Tricks and Crackers, Trigger, Tom and Millie, Trooper, Turdle, Turtle, Virginia Highlander, Walk with Wong, Wanderlust, Ward Leonard, Weightless, Western Canadian Geese, Wildflower, Wildhair, Will-Make-It, Woodsmoke, Woody Pop, Wookie, Youngblood, Zamboni Tow-Step, Zenwalker, Zipper, and Zoo.

The second way was to search out hikers via the Internet before they started hiking and ask them to carry a stack of postcards, and send me notes about where they were, how they were holding up, what was happening to them, etc. I also made postcards available to hikers at places where they are known to gather. Over the course of the project I received some 215 postcards from hikers. Occasionally I was fortunate enough to meet the hikers who sent me postcards somewhere along the way (they are noted above). Some of them I never met but kept up with them via cards and other hikers. These hikers include Alabama Love Bugs, A Quanee, A Wink and A Smile, Bag Lady, Bandanna Light, BB and the Purple Pirate, Betty Crocker, Blue Sky, Chicken Little, Crazy Legs, Cygnus Swan, Double Eagle, Edsel, Gadget, Garbage Disposal, Grim, Heyokay, Landshark, Matt and Tracey, Medusa, Mouse, Ranger Dave, Roses, Skye, Sneakers, Sprout, Steve and Lea, Sundance, Tadpole, Think About it, Thunder and Lightning, Twinkie the Kid, and Zuma.

A third method was to hike along the Trail to visit shelters and other Appalachian Trail Conference facilities and then pilfer comments that had been written in the Trail registers. Since hikers are forewarned that journalists occasionally do this for stories in the local papers, I happily read and lifted comments also. Facilities that I visited included Amicalola Ranger Station, Amicalola shelter and Springer Mountain shelter, Georgia; Wesser Bald shelter, the NOC, the Fontana Hilton, and Mt. Collins shelter, North Carolina; Mount Rogers Outfitters, Wilburn Ridge shelter, Bearfence Mountain hut, Virginia; ATC main office in Harper's Ferry, West Virginia; ATC office in Boiling Springs, Rausch Gap shelter, PA 501 shelter, Allentown Hiking Club shelter, Kirkridge shelter, all in Pennsylvania; Pochuck Mountain shelter, New Jersey; Morgan Stewart shelter, New York; Kay Wood Lean-to, Massachusetts; Little Bigelow Lean-to, Pleasant Pond Lean-to, Hurd Brook Lean-to, Daicey Pond Lean-to and Katahdin Stream Campground office in Maine.

Hikers whose comments I lifted include (but never met or received a card from): Accorn, Apostle Luke, Apostle John, Artemis, AT Actioneer, Bandit, Beater Bomb and Miss Darby, the Bird, Bones, Brush, Bumble, Canadian Geese, Canine Companions, Catskill Eagle, Centurion, Chuck of the Buns of Steel Band, Cimarron, Cosmo, Crash, Doofus, Dre, Entropy, Fisherking, Foxtrot, Goatman, Just-an-Echo, Godfather, Katama, Kilroy, Let it Be, Lightfoot, Little John, Little Tree, Lone Eagle, Lucky Strike, Maple Leaf, the Mapper, Merlin, Misfit, Monkey Butt, Night Owl, Otter, Paco, Poly + Ester, Raindrop and Hibird, Ryan, Seldom Seen, Shaft, Snowshoes, Snowman, Spectre, Sundog, Sweet Pea, Turbo, and Wayfaring Man. Of course, I had heard of many of these hikers from hikers I had met.

A fourth method was to pick up Internet posts from hikers who were posting to an AT list, either during their hikes or just afterward. These hikers include Download and Nexmo, Glider, Gutsy, Sir Goober Peas, and Waldo. Their posts often contained stories about fellow hikers too.

A fifth way was provided by Trail Gimp, who shared her Trail diary with me.

Finally there are the hikers I knew about and probably saw along the way, though we never met: Annie and the Salesman, Big Dipper, Blue Iggy, Buffalo, Hikin' Mike, Iron Phil, MacGuyver, Singe, Slaphappy, Skunktamer, Speedo, Tank, and Walkie-Talkie.

Along the way I also gave rides to several hikers, gave away a lot of calorie-loaded muffins, took one hiker to the hospital, slackpacked a few, helped another board his dog at a kennel, met several parents and spouses, and corresponded with the wife of another.

It was a wonderful summer, one that I will savor for a long, long time.

Lynn Setzer
1996

Occasionally an idea takes hold of a people and assumes a powerful life of its own: King Arthur's Camelot, the New World, the American West. Ideas like these become powerful in part because they hold forth the promise of change, of a fresh start. They inspire people to reach for, discover and build upon the better, stronger, more compassionate part of themselves. Today, the Appalachian Trail has graduated to such a stature.

There are other long distance hiking trails in America, to be sure, but none has captured the American imagination, indeed the international imagination, in quite the same way that the Appalachian Trail has. If all people wanted to do was to take a hike, any trail in any state or national park or forest would do. America offers a lot of them. But the Appalachian Trail is much more than a walk in the woods.

Two thousand, one hundred fifty-eight miles long, the Appalachian Trail follows a path from Springer Mountain, Georgia, to Mt. Katahdin, Maine. It lies within a day's drive of 67 percent of America's population. It passes through many little towns and communities, the kind with friendly people and family warmth, that seem to be disappearing all too rapidly these days. Maintained mostly by people who don't receive money for their efforts, it serves as touchstone to a community of hikers that is incredibly positive and, at times, wickedly funny.

The Appalachian Trail was first conceived by Benton MacKaye (rhymes with *sky*) in 1921. Writing in the *Journal of the American Institute of Architects*, MacKaye noted that "something has been going on these past few strenuous years which in the din of war and general upheaval, has been somewhat lost from the public mind. It is the slow quiet development of the recreational camp. It is something neither urban nor rural. It escapes the hecticness of the one, and the loneliness of the other. And it escapes also the common curse of both—the high-powered tension of the economic scramble." To MacKaye's mind, "playgrounds for the people" along the Appalachian skyline were needed. The mountains would be perfect for recreation, health, fresh air, perspective.

The Appalachian Trail Conference, a private, non-profit organization of clubs and 22,500-plus individual, family, and corporate members that supports MacKaye's dream, estimated *15 years ago* that between three and four million hikers came to the Trail yearly to hike. This, in the days before corporate downsizing, McJobs, and point and click pace of life. Amazing the foresight MacKaye had! The Appalachian Trail, arguably America's most significant sanity check, does indeed provide a way for people to immerse themselves in the beauty of Nature, meet other like-minded souls, challenge themselves, unjangle their nerves and collect their wits. Someone, somewhere is on the Trail every day of the year.

Each year some hikers come to the Trail to attempt a thru-hike, the endeavor of hiking it in a single, generally uninterrupted season. Maybe 20 percent who start will accomplish their undertaking. The rest either quit because they are not ready for the test, sustain major injury, fall sick or experience family emergencies that force them from the Trail.

Once generally the domain of introverted solitude lovers, thru-hiking the Appalachian Trail today has reached incredible numbers. The growing numbers who come out each year—now pushing into the thousands—attest to this fact. One thru-hiker, Wanderlust, observed that "they should change the name from a National Scenic Trail to a National Social Trail."

If you ask a hiker why he or she would want to attempt a thru-hike, you'll get an understandable answer. For many, hiking the Appalachian Trail promises the opportunity to rethink their lives. Something somewhere is askew and they need a time-out from the merry-go-round they are riding. For others, the Trail promises an extended break from the trappings of modern life—technology, asphalt, concrete, clocks—that aren't very pretty and seem somehow to have gotten the upper hand.

(When was the last time anybody you know stood back and said, "Wow! Look at that parking deck! That is *so* beautiful!") For still others, there is the promise of warmth and friendliness and openness of the Trail community, not the office politics, not the backbiting, not the garden variety rudeness, and not the twisted behavior that results when people limbo beneath the weight of legislated niceness. While some people may operate under the assumption that the Appalachian Trail is home to an *Animal House*-like atmosphere, the majority of thru-hikers are serious about their endeavor. For a generation that cut its teeth on Madison Avenue notions that you're likable only when you've bought the right image and smell nice, what thru-hikers learn about themselves and the world around them is spiritually refreshing. You've come a long way, baby, when you realize it ain't what you've bought, it's what you're made of.

What they learn occurs within the context of intense physical and psychological challenges that hiking the Appalachian Trail inevitably presents. As much as the social aspect has dramatically changed the Trail experience, some things have not changed. The elevation gains and losses still wreak havoc on the knees, the packs are still heavy regardless of what a hiker does to lighten the load, it still rains more than every hiker thinks he or she deserves, the bugs still bite mercilessly. And after the first 100 or so miles, the hikers are perpetually and deep-in-their-gut hungry. Do they think about quitting? You bet. Thru-hiking the Appalachian Trail is not a hand-out accomplishment.

So why would anybody want to endure such apparent torture?

After listening to hikers, eating with them, bunking with them and watching them, I believe that the thru-hiking experience strikes a uniquely American chord, one that may only exist in the myths we Americans want to believe about ourselves. I saw it and felt it one evening in Massachusetts.

After talking for 30 minutes or so with two thru-hikers, Scout and Seadog, on the benches outside the lodge at Mt. Greylock, we said our good-byes. They had a few more miles they wanted to put in before they called it an evening. I wished them luck and we parted.

A few minutes later I chanced to look out of an open window and saw them, some 30 yards away, walking up the path to cross Mt. Greylock summit. Scout stopped to adjust her ball cap; Seadog took a bounce step on one foot to bump her pack to its riding position. About 10 yards apart, alone but together, they walked up to the summit. Behind them the sun was turning flame coral; before them the evening sky glowed pink. The evening star glistened and a breeze rolled over the mountain.

They descended into the evergreens, breathing air perfumed by the trees. They left behind schedules, noise—a host of contemporary ills—and walked into life governed by other rhythms. The moment nearly overpowered me and I fought the urge to run out and say, "Wait! Wait! Let me come too!" Maybe Huck and Jim never really rafted down the Mississippi and maybe cowboys never did ride off into the sunset after good deeds done, but on the Appalachian Trail thru-hikers discover something just as good, and probably better. It is a simple, real freedom governed only by things that aren't negotiable: hunger born of real exertion, fatigue that follows a daily determined effort, pride from meeting a challenge, joy that results as the burden of artificiality is stripped away.

This book is crowded in the best sense with the voices of 367 hikers talking about their experiences as they hiked from Springer Mountain, Georgia, to Mt. Katahdin, Maine. Many of the stories were captured before the romance of time could color them. If there are any "stretchers" in here, as Huck would call them, chalk it up to the creativity of the thru-hikers. Separated from the things that have turned much of America into a docile, passive, whining audience, the hikers are remarkably thoughtful, inventive, and verbal. Their comments should serve as a wake up call to national leadership that, as the industrial age gives way to the technological, people are as hungry and needy as ever for the peace that protected wild lands provide. Reasonable, balanced lives simply cannot be had in the parking lots of discount stores or in the dead-end cul-de-sacs of planned unit developments. (Technology is going to come whether we want it to or not; what *isn't* going to happen is the sudden and delightful creation of new, unspoiled wilderness where a person can take a breather.)

A thru-hike, then, is all of this that you will read, and as hikers will tell you, it is even more. Whatever each hiker's experience comes to be is uniquely shaped by what that hiker brings to the Trail. Each hiker brings his or her own set of physical and mental strengths and weaknesses, fears and confidences, quirks and biases. Mix in the variation of weather, time of day, time of year, and other people on the Trail, and the hiker will own a rich and deeply textured experience forever.

A season on the
APPALACHIAN TRAIL

Previous page: Marker at the approach trail to AT, Amicalola Ranger Station, Georgia.

There is a time in every man's education when he arrives at the conviction that envy is ignorance; that imitation is suicide; that he must take himself for better or worse as his portion; that though the universe is full of good, no kernel of nourishing corn can come to him but through his toil bestowed on that plot of ground which is given to him to till. The power which resides in him is new in nature, and none but he knows what that is which he can do, nor does he know until he has tried.

From *Self Reliance*
Ralph Waldo Emerson

m a r c h

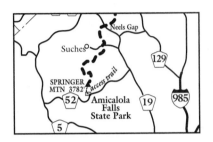

WHO'S ON THE AT IN THIS?

GOD HEP 'EM.

-Soleman

A s February came to a close, spring looked to be in the air, finally. At Springer Mountain, the hallowed ground in north Georgia, daytime temperatures were climbing into the high 40s, nighttime lows dipping only into the high 30s. The first few days of March held the promise of another early spring.

A small wave of hikers had already started on their journey northward, the first registered thru-hiker leaving Amicalola State Park in Georgia on January 4. More followed in February. Their comments about the weather indicated no surprise. They expected the weather to be cold and it was. "My hands are froze," wrote Lightfoot in the Georgia Appalachian Trail Club register. Hat Man and Loco Lobo echoed that observation on January 19 with the report that it was "windy and 0 degrees since 1 P.M." Several days later, Angst wrote, "My God it is Cold." Others were already thinking about their blisters. Raindrop and Hibird thought "about buying stock in moleskin."

Winter in the north Georgia mountains can be a peculiar thing. This portion of the Appalachians does not have quite the elevation of the Smokies—peaks range in the high 3,000s to upper 4,000s—and it is farther south. It is a land where fall lingers, spring arrives early, and winter can be mercifully short. In 1996, however, winter had been brutal. Heavy snows and ice storms had pummeled the area, twisty-curvy roads were often impassable, and roadside waterfalls froze into walls of gray ice.

But that was January and February. Now the red Georgia mud was thawing, and ruts, good sized and deep, were being worn into the Forest Service roads, particularly USFS 42. From across the country and world, optimistic and eager hikers converged upon Amicalola, many with reasons they themselves didn't fully understand, in order to walk that Appalachian roller coaster known in the hearts of many as the "AT." Some, like the Canine Companions, had been planning their hike for three years. Eric Norgaard echoed that sentiment at Amicalola, writing, "no more waiting." Little John wrote that if he "made it today, [he'd] make it all of the way!" Lea Cutter's assessment simply was, "Yikes!"

Though the original idea for an Appalachian Trail neither included nor excluded what has become known as a thru-hike, each year, especially since the early 1980s, one to two thousand hikers converge upon Springer Mountain to try to hike in a single season from Springer Mountain, Georgia, to Mt. Katahdin, Maine, a distance of 2,158 miles. Some who come out are experienced long-distance hikers; some, however, have never slept outside before. Most fall somewhere in between.

As would-be Appalachian Trail thru-hikers wait for the Visitor Center at Amicalola to open so that they might sign the first of many Trail registers, their actions fairly shout out their enthusiasm. Hikers, dressed in all manners of outdoorsy clothing and sporting all manners of lug-sole boots, mill around like ants working bread crumbs. Some step from side

One blaze down and a lot more to go. Springer Mountain, Georgia.

to side, others tap on the stone steps of the sidewalk. Some stretch out their backs and waists, others their calves. Some just bounce up and down. Some peer into the distance looking for Springer Mountain, the southern terminus of this Appalachian Trail they are about to hike. Only a few remain entirely self-possessed, and even many of them look wary.

Loaded backpacks in vivid purples, blues, greens, blacks, and earth-tones—most of them clean—lean against car bumpers, decorating them. So many things—insulated mugs, tiny compasses, thermometers—hang from 'biners that you'd swear the hikers are really peddlers going out to sell their wares. Many hikers extend a hand to other Capilene gypsies, calling out, "Are you starting out today? Are you starting out today?" Come the answers across the parking lot: "Yeah, let's go to Maine!" "Let's do it!" Comments on pack weight fly through the air: "What does yours weigh? Mine weighs 55 pounds." "Mine weighs 63 pounds!" "Mine weighs 47 pounds!" "I don't want to know how much mine weighs!" Some tote their packs to the scale behind the Visitor Center for a final check. Some make a quick trip or two around the corner to the bathrooms. It may be as much as 38 miles by foot before they see flush toilets again. Many hikers cut their eyes furtively, sizing up each other and the respective gear. Who's got good gear? Who's got the best gear? How does my gear compare with his gear? With her gear? Broad but nervous smiles brighten their faces, because for many this endeavor, this attempt to hike the AT, represents a dream of a lifetime.

"How many mail drops do you have?" "Twenty-four" and "26" come back the replies. Mail drops, packages of food and other necessary items that a support person back home sends to post offices in towns on or near the Trail, indicate who has been planning and who hasn't. Hikers with no mail drops—or very few—must surely know all of the tricks of success, or so the rookies think. Still, as hikers will learn, how well the mail drops have been planned or how many of them a hiker has does not ensure success.

"Where's your first one?"

"Walasi-Yi Center."

"Mine, too."

"Suches."

"Oh yeah?"

"Yeah. Pack weight, y'know."

"I got butterflies."

"Yeah, me too."

"I hope I can make it."

"Oh, you'll make it. We're all gonna make it."

"Have you seen the Falls? Are you gonna hike to the Falls?"

"Nah, I'm going to hitch a ride to the top."

"Are they open yet?"

"What time is it?"

"They gotta be here soon! I gotta go hike!"

Some hikers introduce themselves by name, others by a Trail name they have already chosen for themselves. Parents and friends hang close by, friends laughing nervously and parents stealing glances at their children. By now, the arguments for and against this hike have been made, and if there's not enthusiasm radiating from the parents or spouses, there is, at least, acceptance. Mothers reach out to touch their children. Fathers cram their hands in their pockets and size up the crowd from the corners of their eyes. Husbands and wives go through a subtle but nonetheless real separation dance. One moment they stand close to each other as if they don't want to say good-bye and then the next minute the hiking spouse wanders off, introducing him or herself to other hikers. Friends make plans to meet, perhaps, somewhere along the way. Hikers who arrive by themselves without benefit of a friend to distract them, simply sign the register and go. Like Sandman, who traveled first by plane, then by bus, and then finally by cab to reach Amicalola, they may write in their journal, "I sat in a bus station with no one I knew, going to no one I know, in a place I've never been before." There's nothing, short of putting one foot in front of another and moving northward up the Trail, that they can do to make their insides quit churning.

When the ranger does arrive, the group falls silent. It's time. It's really time. The moment of the dream, this dream to follow the two-by-six-inch white blazes marking a seemingly deceptively simple, woodland footpath to Maine, is upon them. The hikers become so quiet that the sound of the ranger unlocking the door reverberates throughout the front yard of the station.

Inside the Visitor Center, hikers write their names, addresses, and pack weight in the Trail register. Remarks such as "Hi ho! Hi ho! It's off to Maine I go!" "Ye-haa!" and "hmmmmm" begin to fill the book. Some hikers, either unsure of their ability or very non-committal, write simply, "I'm going as far as I can." They know that the statistics for success are against them. Parents buy poster-sized maps that show the AT state by state in order to track their children's progress. Friends stand close by not knowing what to do. Eventually they strike up conversations with others about how much they ate at the breakfast buffet in Amicalola Lodge. Non-hiking spouses size up the company of hikers that their loved ones are about to join. Park rangers size up all of the hikers, making mental notes about who they think will make it to Katahdin, about who will not.

The Amicalola rangers have greeted thousands of hikers. "You can just about outfit yourself with the stuff we find on the approach trail to Springer. Sleeping bags, always extra socks. Why once we found this huge jar of peanut butter," noted Kristy Strickland, a ranger there. This send-off drama in and outside the ranger station is repeated nearly every day from March until May and has as much ceremony as a church wedding. For Ralph and Alice, The Honeymooners, it was a part of their wedding. After planning their thru-hike for one and a half years, they were married at the reflecting pond at Amicalola Falls and two hours later left on their hiking honeymoon, with a sign saying "Just" on one backpack and "Married" on the other.

It isn't only the seasonal crop of hikers who are infected with this inexplicable enthusiasm. Former and future thru-hikers catch a little bug called Springer Fever. At home this year, unable to hike, they yearn mightily for the Trail. With other home- and work-bound hikers, they curse their inability to get to the woods. Occasionally a former thru-hiker stricken with a case of Springer Fever will hike to Springer Mountain just to be a part of the send-off, to be a part of the migration again.

One former thru-hiker did just that on March 3. Writing later about that day, he noted, "Twelve years to the date since I started my journey of the path. Today was beautiful, sunny, 50s, and looked very promising, unlike the seven days of rain that kicked my . . . journey off . . . I was surprised at the number of thru-hikers already on the trail. Back then I was one of 10 . . . What a variety . . . two of the Bluegrass Boys, the elder and the younger. At age 79 he is on his second trip up the trail with his grandson. (The first time was age 70.) I was amazed, his love of the mountains and thorough understanding of the physical and mental journey ahead. Three mature women (all in their 60s) planning a thru. Several youngsters and a young couple. Some of these hikers seemed to have no clue what they were in for. It was almost painful to think of the trials ahead of them. My only words of wisdom were to choose their own path, and follow it at their own pace. Once you begin, it's a trail you can truly wander your whole lifetime."

In those first early warm days of March, over 60 hikers left Amicalola bound for Katahdin. Firefly wrote that she was "telling herself that her pack weighs 40 pounds." The Honeymooners noted that "inch by inch, life's a cinch." Others, not yet christened with a Trail name, followed. These hikers joined those who were already walking, including EZ Duz It, Sundog, No-Butt, and Squirrel. This year's hikers had started earlier than ever before, hoping to beat the crowds that were coming in the days ahead. "FINALLY," described the feeling that most of the hikers harbored. But the hikers who expected to be ahead of the crowds were surprised. When H arrived on Springer Mountain, "the shelter was full and there were 10 tents nearby. So I went to the next shelter. It was full too, so I just ended up tenting away from that."

Even though the hikers' spirits were high and their dreams romantic, the AT shows no mercy, for it is not a merciful trail. As hikers quickly learn, there is simply no level ground in Georgia. The approach trail is tough, even when you dodge the first mile—and nearly 1,000 feet in elevation gain—by starting at the top of Amicalola Falls. First it's up to Frosty Mountain, then it's down to Nimblewill Gap. Then it's up to Black Mountain and down to the Black Mountain shelter. Then it's up again to Springer Mountain, where Appalachian Trail and its white blazes begin. Altogether there's about 2,650 feet of elevation gain, just from Amicalola Falls.

Rounded out by tree cover, Springer Mountain looks deceptively friendly. Hikers who have seen pictures of Katahdin know it looks like a monument rising up out of the Maine woods. By comparison, Springer looks like a simple, rounded mound of dirt tucked in among other hills, not distinct, not noteworthy. But elevation maps show another picture: the AT in Georgia follows a sawtooth path up and down and up and down the mountains of the Chattahoochee National Forest toward North Carolina. "No level ground . . . no level ground . . . no level ground," wrote Download, as thru-hikers Nexmo, Cookie, Dusty, MacGuyver, Q-Tip, Yoda, Turtle, Yoda, and ET discovered. The terrain takes its toll early on hikers who are not conditioned to carry heavy packs, which is just about everybody. At Hawk's Mountain shelter, Download noted, "15 exhausted people do not make for a party." Even hikers who go to the gym to condition themselves struggle because, as thru-hikers from previous years will flatly tell you, "nothing prepares you for hiking miles and miles with a 40 pound pack, other than hiking miles and miles with a 40 pound pack." And many hikers, especially in the beginning, try to carry way more than that. Allgood started with 80 pounds.

The Georgia Appalachian Trail Club advises that there is a "potential" for severe weather in the north Georgia mountains in March and that hikers should wait until at least mid-month before starting a thru-hike. For the early hikers, this potential became reality. On March 6, the daytime highs had reached to the 60s. What could be better for hiking? But as arctic air pushed southward, the skies opened up, and during the next two days nearly 4.5 inches of rain drenched the thru-hikers. By Friday it was obvious that winter was not ready to let go. Temperatures dropped brutally low. The highs were merely teasing 30s. The rain turned to snow, and still the temperatures plummeted. On Saturday, the blast brought highs in the 20s, lows in the single digits, if even that much at the higher elevations, and a brutal wind-chill, forecasted to be between -20 to -30. It was the kind of cold that stings in the corners of your mouth and freezes your breath onto your eyelashes. It was the kind of cold that makes your teeth hurt. Out on the Trail, thru-hikers were unaware that they were hiking through some of the coldest temperatures ever recorded during this time of year on this part of the Appalachian Trail.

That kind of cold makes hiking—and life associated with hiking—darned inconvenient. Gearmaster found that after the torrential rains had drenched everything he carried, the plummeting temperatures froze it all. He couldn't unfold his maps or open his trail book—they were frozen shut—his stove was frozen, his boots were frozen and even the cheese he carried in his pack was frozen. The Honeymooners, hikers from Florida who had left Springer only days before, arrived in Gooch Gap and decided to stay in the shelter. It was obvious the front was coming in. "We now know we would have been warmer in our tent," Alice said. But they ate quickly, put on all of their clothes including their rain suits and jumped into their sleeping bags. "Another mistake—the less clothing, the warmer you stay." When they woke up the next morning, "there were two inches of snow on their sleeping bags, the temperature was 5 degrees and the wind-chill was down to -36. We were so cold, and we knew that we needed to get up and move right away. Ralph went to the privy first, and as he needed a free hand, he removed his glove and held it in his teeth." But Ralph's teeth were chattering mightily, and out fell the glove, right straight down into the privy. The Honeymooners found two sticks and after much effort fished the glove back out to daylight. It wasn't funny at the time, Alice said, but there was a positive note: it was so cold, that everything, indeed *everything everywhere*, was frozen.

Many of the hikers came out of the woods just in time. Some reached Suches, while others came down the wet, rocky face of Blood Mountain to Walasi-Yi Center at Neels Gap before the heavy rain and cold turned the world to ice. Sliding down Blood Mountain wasn't an option; with the mountain having such a steep face, a hiker might just slip to his death.

Squirrel, a thru-hiker who had left Springer in February, came walking up at Wesser, his water bottle frozen to ice, as it had been the day before. Squirrel was looking for a bunk to dodge the cold for a day or so. With him was Peter from Damascus who was camping in a bivy sack in the Rufus Morgan shelter waiting to meet a thru-hiking buddy, Little John. Little John was nowhere to be found. Squirrel hadn't seen him, although he told of a Trail Angel in Franklin who parked his pickup at an AT road crossing waiting for a thru-hiker, any thru-hiker, to emerge just so that he could take the hiker to his home and get the hiker out of the bitter cold. In Franklin, Just-an-Echo passed out from hypothermia at Siler Bald shelter and might have died were he not rescued by two other hikers, one of whom happened to be a paramedic. Trail Angels, so named by thru-hikers because these people appear out of nowhere and render a spontaneous and often much needed and always much appreciated kindness to thru-hikers, had ample opportunity to make early appearances in 1996.

Hikers who left Amicalola during the first week of March were also suffering. Although their spirits were high—"We were welcomed to the trail by rain, cold, and rummaging trail mice," wrote Lucky Strike and "Yahoo—Here we go!" exclaimed Stretch—one woman collapsed from hypothermia and was taken from the trail. From Springer Mountain to Fontana Dam, hikers were driven from the trail. Although there wasn't much snow associated with the front at most elevations, the temperatures and wind chill made it a deathly proposition for anyone to hike. Few hikers had come to Georgia prepared for this kind of cold.

Of course, hanging out in Neels Gap waiting for the weather to improve isn't all bad.

After hikers have been on the Trail for some three or four days, just seeing the stone-built Walasi-Yi Center is cause for celebration, for it is there that hikers can get their first hot shower—heaven!—and drink a Coke. To a hiker, the warmth and dryness of the hostel means home, and the cozy, cavernous bunkroom becomes a great place to subdue the dazed, deer-in-the-headlights expression that many of them wear. "Best shower I ever had," wrote Sprout. It doesn't hurt either that Jeff and Dorothy Hansen, managers of Walasi-Yi Center, leave the hostel light on. Of course, coming down from Blood Mountain, most hikers hear the Center before they actually see it. After a few days in the woods, hikers find that the roaring trucks downshifting gears is a wonderful noise, for it tells them that civilization is nearby. Within moments Walasi-Yi Center appears.

Walasi-Yi Center—hiker hostel and first mail drop. Neels Gap, Georgia.

Walasi-Yi Center swirls with comfort, advice, friendship, UPS pickups and drop-offs, curious onlookers, and retail sales. Some hikers are starved for junk food; where are the Cokes? Hikers who started out in jeans and flannel shirts had found that cotton wasn't working. Sweat-soaked cotton made them cold, weighed them down. Purchases for Capilene kept the registers humming. Shoulders and backs hurt like the dickens; is a new pack in order? Feet have black toes and blisters from hammering inside ill-fitting boots on the downhill hauls; are new boots in order? Roses decided that insoles would help his sore feet. And what about walking sticks? Would that take the pressure off the knees? How about different socks? Would that prevent these monster blisters? Jeff and Dorothy and their able, smiling, helpful staff dispense advice and encouragement, direct hikers to the Ben and Jerry's, and help them learn how to pack a backpack.

They also show hikers how to more effectively use the gear they have. "Don't be too proud to ask for a pack adjustment," suggested Centurion. "How do I keep the hip belts from rubbing my hip bones raw?" hikers ask. "Do you know how to do the cross-over?" a staff member replies. Some thru-hikers became quite angry with their gear and accused packs of "not performing." Having bought top-dollar gear, some hikers were reluctant to face a major reality about thru-hiking: it's a daily ration of pain.

For many hikers, the Center is where they pick up their first major mail drop. Whatever the first 38 miles of the AT grinds out of the hikers, the mail drop puts back in, for it is an obvious sign of progress. For other hikers, the Center is where they rethink how much weight they are toting in their packs.

The gear that the hikers carry is a microcosm of life as the rest of the world knows it. Their car is a pair of lug-soled hiking boots and maybe a set of hiking sticks. Their home is a backpack. Their bedroom is a tent, unless they decide to hike the required miles every day to reach the shelters, which are located roughly a day's hike apart. Their bed is a combination of sleeping bag and some sort of pad either to insulate them from the ground or to soften the wooden shelter bunks on which their unroll their sleeping bags. Their kitchen consists of a single burner stove, a fuel bottle, a small pot with a lid and a

Mail drops are the thru-hikers' lifeline.
Walasi-Yi Center, Georgia.

plastic spoon, along with a water filter, iodine tablets for use if the filter breaks, and a water bottle or two. Their pantry is a stuffsack and a rope to hang it away from marauding bears and mice, and they typically allow themselves about a pound of food per day in the beginning. All non-essential packaging is pitched to lessen pack weight. Their bathroom and toiletries consist of a toothbrush—possibly with the handle sawed off to lessen pack weight—toothpaste maybe, dental floss, nail clippers and toilet paper removed from the paper holder—again, pack weight—a lighter and a trowel. Their "medicine cabinet" probably contains vitamins, ibuprofen, bug repellent, moleskin, soap, Vaseline, and maybe a razor. Their tool box consists of a pocket knife, a flashlight, and a spare bulb. Their library consists of trail maps, a data book that notes Trail landmarks, and perhaps a Trail reference book. The hiker's wardrobe consists of rain gear, at least one hat, long underwear, shorts, socks, and a fleece jacket or maybe a wool sweater. Some hikers carry more. Anything else a hiker carries—a radio, a journal, a camp chair, books, camera, other amusements—is at the discretion of the hiker's back and legs.

Before ever hitting the Trail, most thru-hikers have agonized, some for months, over what gear they should carry. Obsessed with the topic, and rightly so, many have sought advice from any and all credible sources. Just the same, however, many are over prepared. Maybe they don't need six hats or that extra pair of jeans. Maybe it's better if they don't wear outdoorsy flannel shirts like the ones in the catalogs. And who's crazy enough to want to carry deodorant any more? The back screams louder than the nose on a thru-hike. Other hikers rethink the amusements and extra equipment that they have brought. Books are proving useless, and few hikers feel like working a crossword puzzle anyhow. They're too tired, and besides, the other hikers are so interesting. Maybe the cast iron frying pan should go. And the ice ax. It can go too.

Every night, while an exotic blend of cooking smells hung in the air at the Hiker Hostel, hikers organized their myriad ziploc bags and discovered what the not-so-cute shelter mice chewed through. "Watch those mice," warned Doofus. "A mouse found its way into my raincoat pocket, chewed its way through and then chewed through my purifier hose." Each morning as the hikers left Walasi-Yi Center and hit the Trail, at least one and probably all muttered, "God, this pack is heavy." A few hikers, underestimating both the pull of homestrings and the difficulty of the Georgia terrain, called it quits. If this is what the next five months would be like, who needed it?

As the severe temperatures drove hikers off the Trail, the Trail hosts at Neels Gap helped make the hikers comfortable. Keith Baily, down the road at Goose Creek Cabins, and George Case, owner of Blood Mountain cabins, provided warm, dry accommodations to the hikers, something that they sorely needed. Wrote Download, "George gave us three beers—it's a dry county—and movies to watch." Although these hikers were comfortable, others were still out on the trail. "We are really praying for them," wrote Download. Meanwhile Peter paced back and forth at the Nantahala Outdoor Center in Wesser, waiting for his friend Little John to show. Watching the Olympic-hopeful kayakers train in the Nantahala River was all very interesting, but where was his friend? In Franklin, Turtle and Godfather were "enjoying restaurant food until it warms." In Wesser, Night Owl noted that "a day's rest, a hot meal, and sleep in a bed does wonders."

By mid-week the cold loosened its grip, and the time for watching videos and kayakers and for eating restaurant food was over. It was time for the hikers to move on. At the NOC, Snowshoe noted, "Glad to see the weather is finally clearing up." Finally, after waiting for five days, Little John emerged into Wesser from the Trail. Climbing straight up and over Albert Mountain had been tough in the cold and wind. Down at Neels Gap, hikers departed. "Feels good to be making progress again," wrote Download. Hiking, not hanging out, was what they were there for. The human bracelet began creeping again.

Meanwhile at Amicalola, the bracelet of hikers became longer as another wave of hikers left Springer believing that this time winter was just about over. Temperatures indicated as much. Daytime highs were in the upper 50s, nighttime lows in the 40s. There was no rain. Over the next week or so, more than 100 hikers registered at Amicalola and more just went to Springer via USFS 42. Among the hikers were Breaking Wind, Heavy Breather, Lobo's Pet, Golden Eagle, Nomad, Ole Swamper, Pins, CrossStone, and Spectre. Spectre noted that he had spent "four years dreaming, one year planning and had 26 mail drops." While the first wave of hikers was glad to be moving toward the Blueberry Patch, this second wave of hikers prepared at Springer for their trek. "Ya-hoo—here we go!" exclaimed Stretch. "The waiting is finally over," commented Maple Leaf. Bandit, who was back for a second try wrote, "I beat this mountain again. Maine bound, hopefully all the way this time." Not all hikers were elated; "Good start—lost my staff and water bottle already," noted Packmule. Some were amazed that they were even on the Trail. Noted Fisherking,

"62 years old. Lordy, Lordy." Others wrote encouragement to themselves and to the others who were to follow, "One step at a time," cautioned Turtle. But once again the hikers quickly saw that hiking to Springer Mountain is tough. Wrote one hiker after the day's haul, "Lone Eagle has arrived. Tired."

But the weather had not cleared up; it was only a tease. Winter decided once again to challenge the hikers. From Springer Mountain to the Smokies, rain slowed the hikers and then heavy snow trapped them. On March 19, Nature turned seriously challenging. Arriving at Springer Mountain on March 20, a hiker noted, "I was looking for a warm place to sleep. I'm still looking." Spending her first night on Springer, Mosey lay in her sleeping bag and thought quietly, "I'm going to die and nobody will ever find me." Ryan Erickson observed that "snow was coming down in every direction and that was in the shelter."

The Honeymooners had reached Standing Indian Mountain and had finished dinner as the rain started. Tired, they crawled inside their tent. However, just before drifting off to sleep, Ralph noticed a change in the sound of the rain. It had turned to sleet. During the night the sleet turned to snow, something Alice discovered as she decided to go out to relieve herself. "I didn't want to put my boots on, so I decided to do as a hiking friend of mine and use a ziploc bag. It worked great. But as I was zipping it up to place outside the tent, I realized there was a hole in the bag. What a disaster." Getting up the next morning, they realized that the snow had continued to fall. "We decided to wait it out, assuming it wouldn't last much longer. We ate breakfast and went back to sleep, ate lunch and went back to sleep. It was still snowing. Now it was about 10–12 inches deep. We ate dinner and went to sleep and it was still snowing. During the night we decided to get up every hour to shake the snow off our tent, as it was a three-season tent and couldn't take the weight."

"At about 2:00 A.M., Ralph shook the tent and shortly after he had trouble breathing. He asked if I were OK. I was real short of breath, too. Evidently, the snow had piled up so high, about 18 inches, that it cut off the air flow through the tent. Ralph had to go dig a trench around the tent so we could breathe. We kept shaking the tent and keeping the airflow open all night. It was still snowing in the morning and I was worried. With 18–20 inches of snow and drifts even higher, there was no way of seeing the Trail.

"Around noon, and still snowing, two thru-hikers, Quiet Man and Home Brew, were breaking through snow to come down Standing Indian to find their way out. I heard them and blew a whistle. They came by and told us they were getting out—snow was too high. We checked the map and saw that the forest road next to our campsite was about six miles from a major road leading to Franklin, NC." Seeing that this was their best chance to get out while other hikers were helping to cut a trail, The Honeymooners packed up and left. Following the tire tracks of a forest service vehicle to the main road, they were picked up by a Trail Angel who took them into Franklin. There The Honeymooners joined company with 22 other hikers. While waiting out the storm in Franklin, Home Brew found himself stranded in a dry town. "I came up with the idea of brewing beer on the Trail. I did some experimenting and after brewing my first batch, it seemed feasible. Hopefully I will be able to provide thirsty hikers with beer on my journey north."

Gumby, who was caught in the two feet deep snow at Siler Bald, thought about how he almost didn't bring a hat and gloves with him. "I'm from up north and I never thought that in March it would be that cold down South." A Wink and A Smile tried to leave the Nantahala Outdoor Center, "but the weather turned us back."

Hikers in the Smokies experienced the worst of it. Aunt Jemima and Sir Goober Peas were just entering the Smokies. "We knew the forecast . . . sounded simple enough . . . 6–8 inches of snow. We could handle that, no problem. We left the Fontana Hilton and headed into the Smokies. Before we crossed the dam, we ran into Walkie-Talkie, a older hiker who

Looking into the snowy Smokies. Fontana Lake, North Carolina.

was clearly giving a great deal of weight to the weatherman's predictions. He shouted at us 'you fellas need your heads examined' when we told him of our plans. As we climbed up Shuckstack, the wind blew and the snow came down in dense sheets. We were thrown off course by the 'new' ground cover and several large blow downs left from Opal. There were only a couple of inches of snow on the ground when things seemed to taper off, and I again felt the sense of disappointment that the weather forecast had blown the storm completely out of proportion.

"We were loaded down with nine days of food and by the next morning, it was snowing again, the kind of steady accumulation that you know will add up to a couple of feet before long. We were headed a mere seven miles but the snow made it a whole new challenge. We came into Russell Field Shelter in the late afternoon; it was still snowing heavily.

"The next morning we were faced with snow that completely covered the tracks of those a day ahead of us. Going to Derrick Knob shelter, we found that the snow in the flat sections of the Trail frequently drifted to our knees. As we ascended the exposed ridge of Rocky Top, AJ and I had to contain our laughter when confronted with waist high drifts. It became easier to walk through the thick brush on the leeward side of the Trail, in order to walk through snow drifts only two feet high.

"There were several times during that week that while we trudged through the snow, I cursed it and the Trail and even my choice to hike the AT."

Gearmaster spent two nights in the restroom at Clingman's Dome with his hiking partner. They pitched their tent inside the ladies' room, while two other hikers spent the night in the janitor's closest and a group of hikers on spring break commandeered the men's room. After having his boots freeze again and again, Gearmaster finally realized that he could sleep with one boot over his heart and the other boot over his groin. "It might have been uncomfortable, but at least my boots didn't keep freezing," he said.

But the hikers hunkered down, looking inward for the strength to keep hiking. It was way too early to give in to negative thinking. "No doubt we were damn cold and miserable at times," said Sir Goober Peas, "but then again we were in charge. We were making ourselves masters of our destiny. Plus this kind of challenge is what the Trail is all about." Hiker efforts to support each other ran the gamut. CrossStone, composing a poem to make the miles go by, shared it with his shelter mates at Blue Mountain, Georgia, and wrote it in the shelter register to cheer the others who would follow.

Welcome To Spring

I met a man headed north on a hike.
I asked him his name 'n what the Trail had been like.

"They call me CrossStone," he said with a smile.
I been hikin' alone now, for quite a while.

"Come up from Springer just a few days ago,
been put through the wringer, but I's still rarin' to go.

"The temperature she dropped to down around 20.
But my friends in the shelter on Springer were plenty.

"My water filter she froze with hardly a warnin'
Broke into 80 pieces about 3 in the morning.

"While the snow kept a fallin' and it got mighty windy
We started to worryin' 'bout losing poor Cindy.

"If you don't believe me, ask someone who knows.
And Matfly will tell you how, he 'most lost seven toes.

So the wind keeps on howling and the temps gettin' colder
But deep in his nest is a mouse gettin' colder.

While shivering he crept, slowly making his rounds
While soundly we slept, he had Snickers and Mounds.

Ryan showed me his pack when I woke in the mornin'
Where the mouse had his snack while we all were snorin'.

"Don't worry, be happy," I said to my friend
For in just a few months we'll all be at the end.

"On Katahdin we'll stop and think of the night
Of the poor freezin' mouse with the case of frostbite.

Other hikers, less poetically inclined, cheered themselves and others with humor as biting as the wind. Bly Gap was reportedly renamed "Camp Cold as Hell." Zamboni Tow-Step was truly grateful for Trail Angel Barry Henley. Zamboni's stove had broken, mainly because it had frozen in the severe temperatures. When Barry showed up with pizza and beer at the Tray Mountain shelter—and swapped his working stove for Zamboni's broken one—Zamboni knew that Trail Angels and the magic they deliver are for real. A Quanee noted that although it was incredibly cold and windy, the weather didn't keep the Blood Mountain shelter skunk from visiting.

From Neels Gap to Wesser, hikers who could exit the trail did so and were grateful for the forced rest. The cold was brutal, and knees and feet were taking an absolute pounding. Firefly saw it as a good opportunity to "heal the feet." Safair and Le Chef wanted to spending the day "recovering from battered knee syndrome." Artemis had come down with the flu. Roses just wanted to dry out: "Everything I own is soaked." At the Blueberry Patch, Gary and Lennie were serving up stacks of their famous blueberry pancakes and helping Yoda nurse the blisters on her feet. Merlin found magic at the Walasi-Yi Center and The Whiner simply praised them by saying, "What a Godsend." Fisherking enjoyed his "warm night in a lovely cabin."

Typical shelter on the Appalachian Trail. Wilburn Ridge Shelter, Virginia.

Hikers who stayed on the Trail, however, enjoyed the ambiance of shelters in the snow. "The soft glow of a few coals and the many packs hanging from the ceiling recalled an ancient castle where medieval nomads sought refuge from the weather and beasts," reflected Sir Goober Peas.

Weather comes and weather goes, and once again, the skies cleared and hikers inched northward. During the last days of March more hikers came to Amicalola to begin their pilgrimage. Kiwi, who had come to Springer twice but decided to hold off because of the weather, was tired of hanging out in Atlanta. It was now or never for his hike. "Grab life by the malt balls," exclaimed Skylark, ready to go. "Don't rain just yet," begged Boldheart. Crunching the brown leaves and walking beside the gray, matchstick trees not yet swollen red with spring, another wave of hikers pushed its way up Springer Mountain.

The calendar may have indicated it was spring, but so what? Spring decided to pick up where winter had left off and socked it to the hikers, this time with rain that alternated between downpours and drizzle. "Great to start if you're a fish," remarked Kick-a-Tree. "Hope they all make it, including me," wrote Catfish. Any of the famous views offered up on the summits was socked in with fog. Clouds raced thick across Blood Mountain, clouds sat at Woody Gap, clouds blanketed the Nantahala Gorge. Any of the famous sunsets was obscured by the same. Hikers in the Smokies slogged up the Trail that was by turns icy or muddy. Still the hikers hiked northward, believing in a reward, convinced that things would get better. Any small reward would serve as motivation to keep going. "I was looking for a warm place to sleep," noted Youngblood. "I'm still looking."

For many hikers, however, the rewards were wet gear, mucky boots, and blisters on their palms worn in from their walking sticks. When Attitude stopped at Walasi-Yi Center, he poured about half a cup of water out of a supposedly waterproof stuffsack. "Look at this," he mumbled to anyone within earshot. Mover and Heavy Breather spent time at Wesser cleaning their boots hoping to prolong them. Getting the mud out might prove to be the difference. Every hostel that housed a hiker was draped with tarps and tents and bags as hikers tried to dry their gear in the soggy air. Like Download, hikers were learning that the Trail was composed of two kinds of mud: "the grab-your-boot-and-yank-it-off kind and the slick-go-for-a-ride kind."

The rewards of pain and fatigue and injury made themselves obvious. Marmot's hip bones were rubbed raw because the hip belt on her pack wasn't broken in. Many hikers had bruised feet from hammering their toes inside their boots on downhill hauls. Nomad summed it up, saying "It's been amazingly draining hiking 8–16 miles a day. At the end of the day, all you really want to do is sleep. I can't remember ever having been as tired every night for such a long time. Every morning it takes from 30 minutes to an hour to get the aches and pains out of the joints. I'm hoping that in another week or so I will start to enjoy more and ache less." Garbage Disposal seconded Nomad's observation, saying "Every vista and every meal is hard fought and well deserved." Mosey, who hadn't died on Springer Mountain after all, was contending with a sore collar bone cause by a pack that rubbed her the wrong way. Mover, her husband, took time off to fashion a lamb's wool pad to ease the rubbing. Many hikers, thinking silently to themselves, echoed Squirrel's complaints. "The Trail is crazy. Why do I have to go to the top of every mountain? Why can't I go around it to get to the shelter?"

Throughout March thru-hikers trekked northward marveling at the damage left behind by Hurricane Opal, a storm that had come through the previous October. Trail volunteers had performed a significant service in clearing the footpath.

Forest rangers from Georgia to North Carolina indicated that in fact March 1996 had not really been a month full of unusually severe weather; rather, it had been full of generally typical March weather. The problem was, the rangers pointed out, that the winters of '94 and '95 had been mild, so by comparison, the '96 hikers thought they were getting tough weather. The warning of the Georgia Appalachian Trail Club was spot on.

Trail rumor held that over 500, maybe even 1,000, hikers had left Springer Mountain in March bound for Mt. Katahdin in Maine. Were they crazy to undertake such an endeavor? Maybe. Why would anybody want to slog through mud or shiver in a sleeping bag at sub-zero temperatures?

What was it that put them on the Trail? What would the hikers say?

Some hikers came to Springer Mountain, because they didn't want their lives to be a collection of "I wish I hads." One hiker said, "I got tired of listening to my father talk about the things he wished he'd done. He's too old now, too frail. And he's angry about it. Rather than have my life turn out like that, I thought I'd give it a try." One hiker simply said that he "was tired of getting partial credit in the exam of life."

For some, the novelty of long distance hiking lured them to the Trail. Who back home would believe it, walking all day, living out of a pack, sleeping in mass at night, meeting just about anybody under the sun? Gilligan had quite an experience when he met The Rabbi in Suches. Although seemingly harmless enough, The Rabbi and his combination of rusted car, coat hangers butterflied together to make a radio antenna and driving skills caused Gilligan to use the Walasi-Yi Center Trail register to caution other hikers about accepting a ride.

The opportunity to choose a new persona motivated others. As Jabberwocky explained, "Out here you can choose who you want to be." Those who do not choose a Trail name are often delighted when circumstances provide one. One hiker, staying at the Blood Mountain shelter, left a warm sleeping bag during the middle of the night to visit the privy. He forgot to zip the bag. Upon returning he found that the resident skunk liked the warm spot too and had nestled down into the bag. The hiker, beginning to shiver, had no recourse but to charm the skunk out of the bag. Miraculously he did so, and Skunktamer was born. Golden Eagle, it turned out, was yellow-blazing, the hiker term for following the center line on the asphalt as he hitchhiked up the Trail. Mailman was named for his 34 mail drops. "I wanted to keep my pack weight light, but you should see what I'm spending in postage!" Home Brew earned his because a friend was sending him homemade beer.

Other hikers enjoyed the challenge in hiking the Trail and learning about its quirks. Wrote Download, "I pushed on to the nearest trail, ignored the data book and dismissed the fact that white blazes were missing. I descended for about .2 of a mile, looking hopefully for the next white blaze. Well, Nexmo prevailed, we climbed back to the top of Cowrock, followed the instructions in the book and continued on the AT. Unfortunately I will be reminded of this for at least a month, but there is a bright side: Nexmo has no weapon."

Some hikers, just recently in the job market and not able to find work, thought six months in the woods seemed like a good idea. Some came because they just didn't want to enter the working world. Other hikers, who had landed jobs the jobs they wanted, had discovered that they now hated those jobs. Women occasionally said that "I've been someone's daughter and I've been someone's wife and I've been someone's employee, but I'm still not sure who I am."

Other hikers came looking for a more personal challenge, and they clearly reveled in the experiences that beset them. Cygnus Swan "started with a pit of embers in [her] gut. I wanted to hike the Trail. But I did not know what fueled the coals. It's dawning now. Out here—nothing is taken for granted." Wrote Barefoot, "I was reminded of the adventure we are undertaking. If you want something, you must be willing to take risks, yet if you truly want something, you must be willing to risk everything. I, for one, would rather crawl to Maine with pride than admit to defeat." Said Chicken Little, "I have learned not to let the wild ups and downs of everyday life touch me and whoever would have thought I could live without the comforts of home! The quest of the mountains and really seeing what I could put my body through at almost 50 years has surprised me. I am so glad I took time out of everyday life to travel up the AT. The reality you experience is a mirror image of your expectations!"

Of course, not all hikers admitted to searching for deep meaning. Wildhair just shrugged and said, "I turned 40." Sandman just laughed and said, "it must have been that kick to the head when I was an infant."

To be sure, some hikers came to the Trail simply to be around others who shared their enjoyment of the simple act of hiking. Evidently a speedster, Hannibal the Brit, who had started early, passed through Harper's Ferry in late February, and reached the Delaware Water Gap in Pennsylvania, decided to turn around and walk back south, just to enjoy the camaraderie of the Trail. It just didn't seem like thru-hiking without other thru-hikers around.

april

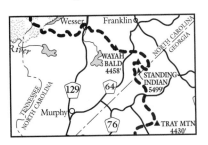

THERE ARE GOOD DAYS

AND BAD DAYS.

- Crazy Legs

April: a month of contradictions. Spring is supposed to arrive, but in 1996 winter clung to the mountaintops. The hikers went to the woods to enjoy rebirth of nature and to have solitude to reflect about themselves and their endeavor. Instead they found hundreds of other hikers. They embarked with their spirits soaring only to find that indeed the flesh can be unwilling. Hikers who left Springer Mountain in March endured the challenges of hiking, some of them accumulating nearly 500 miles, only to realize that they were only little more than a quarter of the way to Maine. On a daily basis they either acclimated, accepted and adapted to Trail life, or they quit. Scout said it best: "There is nothing that can prepare you for this trip, except, of course the willingness to accept all that comes your way, from weather to terrain." It is a hard lesson for many hikers to learn, however.

When hikers greet each other in the shelter with the question, "Do you snore?" they aren't trying to be clever. They're serious. After spending hours hiking, what most hikers want, after food, is sleep. (A shower would be nice, but they're getting used to being grubby. "I was trying to stay clean," laughed Jabberwocky, "but I got over it.") They're tired, real tired, real bone tired. They've just spent the day lugging a 40-plus pound pack up the Trail and when they reach a shelter or hostel, they're ready to spread out the Therm-a-Rest, take the bag out of the stuffsack, unlace and take off the boots, and literally take a load off. Which they do. And it feels good—euphoric, really—until later in the dark when the chainsaws crank up. Hikers who have never slept around others who snore are amazed at the varieties of rhythms. First there is the basic chainsaw, whose pattern sounds something like *aauuuunnnkk-fooooo. . . . aauuuunnnkk-fooooooo. . . . auukKKOW!* Sometimes the sound is more round and hollow, like *ooowwwwwnnnnK! . . . ooowwwwwnnnnK!* Then there is the slightly nasal chainsaw whose snoring sounds something like *eeeuuunnnk-fooooop. . . . eeeuuunnnk-fooooop. . . . eeeuuunnnk-fooooop.* There may even be a chainsaw or two who doesn't really snore at all but rather puffs: *puuuuf. . . . puuuuf. . . . puuuf.* Or maybe the pattern is *pif! . . . pif! . . . pif!* Whoever said repetitive sounds are soothing obviously never shared a shelter with snoring thru-hikers.

The word goes out quickly on the Trail about who snores and who doesn't. For hikers looking forward to some semblance of sleep, nothing spoils it more than hikers who snore. Munchkin almost earned a new trail name—Lizzie Borden—when, after listening to a hiker snore most of the night in one of the Smoky Mountain shelters, she threatened the hiker to within an inch of his life. Laughing about the entire sleepless night, Munchkin knew that "this guy was snoring so loud, that if I killed him no one in that shelter would have reported it. They would have kept it to themselves and thanked me for the sleep they could finally get." Some hikers, trying to respect the chainsaw's right to life and get some sleep at the same time, just get up and move. Others are grateful for their tents. In Hot Springs, North Carolina, at the Jesuit hostel, Midnight seriously thought about taking her bag out to the picnic tables, and would have, except that it was raining. She then considered the hallway but thought she'd likely be stepped on. In the spirit of Trail tolerance, she just endured the rumble. Loon Lady would pass out ear plugs to whoever wanted them, so loudly did her husband snore. Ladybug, after enduring her first sleepless nights on the Trail, was looking forward to a good sleep at the Walasi-Yi Center. But later that evening, the room, she said, "sounded like something from the Three Stooges." Not to be robbed of sleep, Ladybug lay on her bunk a little while and considered how to solve this problem. Then quietly she got up and went to her pack and retrieved the solution. The small OB tampons were better than ear plugs and in the morning she could quickly remove them by tugging on the little string. And did she sleep well? "Oh yeah," she smiled. "No problem."

Occasionally there is a hiking couple who can't seem to go without a nocturnal romp. Again, in the spirit of Trail tolerance and "hiking your own hike," hikers try to ignore the show and get some sleep. Fatigue is stronger than prurient interest. But one couple earned quite a reputation for their appetite, so much so that hikers were describing them as being "just like rabbits." Finally, one night in a shelter, a tired hiker decided to say something. Enough was enough, and so, on behalf of his fellow hikers, the voice of Tank filled the shelter: "Hey guys, it's about sleep. We're here to sleep. OK? Got that? Sleep."

Even if every hiker in the shelter exhibits acceptable shelter etiquette, there is always the Mice Capades to keep hikers awake. Hikers try to be charitable to the little beasts, they really do. "Cute little buggers," laughed Landshark. And Bear attempted a Zen-like attitude saying, "I'm sure that they have a place in the universe." But shelter mice eventually try the patience of every hiker in some way or another and there seem to be gazillions of them.

Because of the mice, just about every shelter looks like a party about to happen. Numerous rusty tuna cans dangle like lampshades from strings tied to the shelter ceiling. But these homegrown streamers aren't meant

Bloody Nose and Bear with anti-mice devices. Wesser Bald Shelter, North Carolina.

for decoration for some rustic party. The theory is that when you reach the shelter, you take your food bag out of your pack and hang it on the string. The mice, having worn little mouse interstates into the rafters, will then run the rafters of the shelter, find a string, run down that string, but be unable to figure out how to get over and around the tuna can without falling off the string. Voila! The food bag is protected and the hiker won't starve.

But that's theory. So many people were thru-hiking in 1996 that shelters looked like smokehouses, the food bags hanging like hams being cured. Food bags were close together, and mice, eager for their next meal, were discovering jumping skills they didn't know they had. Hikers became convinced that the Mouse Internet was carrying the following post: "Don't worry about running down that little string. Just jump, boy! Jump! You'll hit something!" Youngblood believed that during the day the mouse commandos came out to scope the possibilities, took back the data and led the troops back at night for a nighttime blitz.

And of course the little beasts run near you and around you and on you. "All those mice were running along my body, my head, my stuff," noted Sweet Dreams. They're not proud; they're just shelter mice indoctrinating hikers to the joys of the Trail. Jabberwocky, a hiker who slept with jester's cap on to keep his head warm, awoke one night to the sound of teeny tiny feet scratching closer and closer to his head and running up one of the streamers on the cap. He lifted his arm to swat the mouse and successfully nailed him. Fortunately for the mouse—but not so for Jabberwocky—the blow sent the mouse airborne to a streamer next to Jabberwocky's face. The mouse, running for daylight down streamer, jumped into the bag with Jabberwocky, running for the daylight he wasn't going to find.

Windwalker was likewise annoyed with the mice. Gutsy, staying in Blue Mountain shelter, noticed that the "mice had found [Windwalker's] pack and were literally fighting over something in it. Every once in a while, he would reach up with a stick and whack vigorously on his pack. They would be quiet for awhile but then they would start over again." Most hikers don't sleep at all in the beginning of their hikes because they're paranoid about mice getting into their packs.

Over and over again, hikers will find upon waking the next morning, acorns in their boots, little gifts from the shelter mice, because mice do manage, somehow, to get into everything hikers bring into the shelters. Occasionally they'll find gorp in their boots. One hiker, Slaphappy, had the most symbiotic relationship with the shelter mice: one saw fit to give birth to a litter in her pack. Often the mice become a source of entertainment as hikers from the South use the opportunity to torment their new hiker friends from the North. "Yeah, I tell Yankees that shelter mice are reincarnated Southern generals and they're looking for northern hikers, to chew through their packs," laughed Jabberwocky. Occasionally the mice don't fare too well, though. Greenleaf, a "sitar playing minimalist," was trying to learn how to eat mice so that he could live off the Trail, according to Gutsy.

Mice aren't the only critters hikers must contend with on the Trail. There's also the sound of love in the air as grouse-drumming hits its peak in mid-April. Many a thru-hiker has been awakened in the middle of the night thinking he or she was having a heart attack when it was only the grouse drumming in its annual ritual to perpetuate the species. Listening to a grouse take flight "sounds like a motorbike starting," Trail Gimp noted.

To be sure, a thru-hike without grouse drumming and shelter mice running is not really a thru-hike, which is why when the chainsaws appear at the hostels, other hikers' spirits droop just a little. It would be nice to get some real sleep for a change—no mice, no grouse, and no chainsaws. "For religious reasons, I never pass up a motel," Pokey flatly stated. "I want to keep my religion and I want to get some sleep."

For some of the early season hikers, April became a time for quitting. It's just a fact: put a lot of weight on a back and on feet and knees that are not used to it, try to make a lot of miles over unforgiving terrain in weather mean enough to put a bit in your mouth, and something's going to give. Generally it's the hiker. The terrain in Georgia is harder than most hikers expect and North Carolina doesn't get any easier. It doesn't matter how many times they tell themselves and each other that Georgia is "where character is built," the Trail takes its toll. When they wake up in the middle of the night with knees and feet pounding with pain, many hikers realize that hiking the AT is more than a grand, roving, outdoors social event: it's real, physical work that hurts.

By the time hikers arrive in Franklin, North Carolina, many have feet that "look like hamburger," according to Jackie Kussow at Three Eagles Outfitters. "I wonder who sells them their boots," she muses. "You can't imagine the blisters I've seen, even on the tops of their feet. Of course, they're so full of excitement when they get here that they don't care." A glance at hikers' heels and toes, even their palms, might lead the uninformed to think that they're watching hikers transform into Tin Men from Oz: for many hikers, duct tape is the blister solution of choice, and toes and heels and palms sport patches of the silver stuff. Some hikers who try to persevere despite their pain only make it worse, for the blisters become infected.

By the time the hikers arrive in Wesser, knee pain is commonplace. The 2,700 feet downhill haul from Wesser Bald into the Nantahala Gorge only aggravates the problems. "Where was the runaway hiker ramp?" Jarhead asked. Toes often turn a plum-colored black, knee joints swell, tendonitis sets in, and every step screams back.

Hikers devise clever ways to keep hiking through the pain, like Ranger Dave, who tried to hike backward to make the pain stop. Others decide that maybe sidestepping down the mountains will work. Some hikers try to hike straight through with twisted ankles, the result of heavy packs, root-bound and rock-strewn trails, and a step that somehow went wrong. Many women learn how to piddle without squatting because their legs are so sore that they simply cannot squat to answer Nature's call. Sometimes hikers, despite their best efforts—their boots are broken in, the pack is relatively light, the pace is reasonable—are stopped because of other problems. "My foot was getting bigger than my boot," said Loon Lady at Fontana Dam, unsure of what was causing the trouble. For some hikers it's an ingrown toenail caused perhaps, by trimming a nail just a shade too close. Maybe it's a bad fall. Maybe it's a stress fracture. Maybe it's some virus. Whatever it is, some hikers stop along the way to heal, and mercifully they do. Others, after agonizing pro and con conversations inside their heads, stop to heal but decide to stop for good.

When hikers bail this early on the Trail, it can be an emotional, gut-wrenching experience. Nobody expects to quit so soon. Everyone leaves Springer believing that he or she will make it to Katahdin, although every hiker is well aware of the statistics: Only 10–15 percent or so will actually complete a thru-hike in a single season. When they bail because of pain, it's not only the body that hurts. It's the spirit. They brimmed with enthusiasm just a few weeks ago. They had planned so carefully, sometimes for years, before ever arriving in Georgia. But now the body isn't up to the task and their ears are full of doctors' lectures delivered from the emergency clinics of Franklin and Bryson City, North Carolina. Blistered feet open the door to nasty infections. Inflamed knees and muscles can do only so much and continuing to hike on them isn't helping them heal. Regardless of how wise the decision to quit is, it doesn't stop the disappointment of watching one's hiking group disappear on the Trail. "I'm not the hugging type," remarked Rafiki as he stopped in Wesser for a few days to let an injured toe heal. "But it really hurt to watch the last of the group I left Springer with leave. It really hurt." His eyes contained all of the emotion that his voice choked back. Robohiker stopped in Wesser for nearly a week because of foot pain. Trying to stay off of the foot, trying to work through the pain, finally he was able to hike on—and hiked 70 miles in three days to catch up with the group he had started with. Such are the bonds that begin to form.

Other hikers, however, bail with a sense of relief. They never counted on how much work there is in thru-hiking. Nearly everyday the same routine must be followed: get up, eat a bite, pack up, hoist the pack, start walking. Walk a while, enjoy a view if it isn't raining, take a break. Set down the pack. Unpack a snack, sip some water. Pick up the pack, walk a while, take a break. Set down the pack. Unpack a snack, sip some water, loosen the boot laces—got a downhill coming—pick up the pack, walk a while. Walk a while more, take a break. Set down the pack. Unpack a snack, sip some water. Reach the shelter, finally, take off the pack, find the stove, eat something besides gorp—what starchy dinner am I having tonight: rice or pasta? Will it be mac and cheese and tuna or tuna mac and cheese?—wash out the little pot using only the tiniest amount of water, drink some water, hang the food bag, untie the Therm-a-Rest, unroll the bag, get the water filter, walk to the spring, filter the water, walk back to the shelter, sit down, and breathe deeply. Like Blister Free said, "It's a lot like work. I have to get up everyday and walk whether I want to or not." Some start hating their little cookpots. Every day they cook in it, they eat out of it, they wash it out with the tiniest bit of water. Same pot, same spoon. Everyday. For some hikers, this way of living is a drag and there aren't enough Trail towns, Trail magic, Trail angels, or good views to compensate for the grind. And it's worse when it rains—and it rains often.

Some hikers bail because their expectations were never quite in synch with the reality of a thru-hike. This smorgasbord of mud, starchy food, and pain is not what they expected. They arrived at Springer thinking that most days would be sunny, that their gear would work perfectly—after all, hadn't they bought top-dollar packs and boots?—and that they would just cruise from Georgia to Maine, no prob. When they find that often there are no sunny days for maybe five or six or ten in a row, or that expensive gear doesn't level out the Trail and make the walking easy, they're angry. They aren't having fun and nothing is going right. Their feet hurt, their knees hurt, their backs hurt, they smell bad, their gear is wet and heavier than normal and—sweet Jesus—they're eating mac and cheese again. There are other hikers on the Trail they don't understand and whose habits they don't like. They never understood that they would be the ones who would have to adjust—not the Trail or the other hikers. The Appalachian Trail, eternal in its being, timeless in its lure, unfeeling in the experience it delivers, is not impressed by those who think they will conquer it. The AT is not something that exists to be conquered.

The hikers who reach Hot Springs have begun to discover this. After working through blisters, Navigator endured shin splints. "Oh well," he sighed, "it always seems to be something breaking down." Disturbed by the amount of gear they see left on the Trail—in the Smokies Mr. and Mrs. Honeymooner came upon a tent with a note stuck on it, giving the tent to whomever needed it, for the owner had quit—hikers quit talking about their chances of reaching Katahdin. Many are through talking about how much they hurt. They hurt, they know they hurt, and they know that talking about it doesn't do any good. They just quietly swallow their vitamin I—ibuprofen—and go to bed. "What good does it do to focus on it?" asks Midnight. "I just set little goals and accomplish that. I don't even think about Maine." Looking at the AT map on the wall in the kitchen of the Jesuit hostel, she said, "I'd be depressed if I really looked at that map. I've already hiked 270 miles and I have so much more in front of me. But I just can't think like that. I can't pay any attention to how much lies in front of me." Jarhead employed a similar strategy, "I quit thinking about how many miles I was going to do each day. I just quit worrying about it. And you know, I found that once I quit thinking about it, I was making more miles. I was just doing it." Tadpole learned that a "great day of hiking is achieved by taking many breaks."

Cold Finger talked about his expectations of the weather: "Before I ever came out here, I expected that I would be wet about half the time. So far I haven't been disappointed." Buzz noted that "the Trail is not real exciting, but [is] satisfying. Have to get used to being wet and most of your gear being wet." Crazy Legs, who'd had only seven sunny days out of his first 28 on the Trail, summed it up by saying, "Hiking the AT is a lot like life. There are good days and there are bad days. The key is to push through the low days, knowing that you will appreciate the good days that much more." Many hikers try that strategy and find that it works. Others aren't so lucky.

Hikers who stay on the Trail discover that they're turning into eating machines. Bo Knows, a hiker turned Trail Angel, picked up hikers at Newfound Gap and took them to the all you can eat buffet at Duff's in Pigeon Forge. On one occasion he picked up eight hikers, Bull Moose among them. By the end of the dinner, Bo Knows counted 32 empty plates on the table, not including the 17 dessert plates. Five of the dinner plates belonged to Bull Moose.

Pokey recalled listening to Lone Wolf tell how by the end of the hike they'd be eating out of dumpsters, if given the chance. (Lone Wolf was attempting his 10th thru-hike and sharing with the newcomers things he had learned in his previous nine hikes.) In Neels Gap, Pokey mentally dismissed that story, telling himself that he "was a gentleman, and besides, his momma raised him better." Two and a half weeks later, near Fontana Village, Pokey hitched a ride with a young man who had several pizza boxes in the passenger seat of his car. Picking them up, Pokey could tell that they were empty. All, that is, except one. It felt sort of heavy and maybe was it a just a little bit warm? Pokey opened up the pizza box and saw a few slices of pizza.

"This yours?"

"Yeah."

"How old is it?"

"Four hours, maybe."

"You saving this for later?"

"No."

"Sure?'

"Sure."

"Sure?"

"Yeah, sure."

"Mind if I eat this?"

"No, go ahead."

"Sure?"

"Sure."

Swallowing the third bite, Pokey instantly remembered what Lone Wolf had said. He hated to admit it, but maybe dumpsters were in his future after all.

Pilgrim, laughing about his appetite, mentioned that he heard the Hardee's in Hiawasse burned. "I guess I ate too many hamburgers." No Name, after making it to the Fontana Hilton, was talking about hikers who consider carrying guns for protection. "I can't imagine doing that. Do you know how much food the weight of a gun equals?"

Thru-hikers amuse themselves talking about their growing appetites. Jarhead ribbed Medicine Woman, saying, "It's been 15 minutes since you ate anything." To which she replied, "You know, you're right," and pulled out some gorp and ate a handful. The standard measure of distinguishing types of hikers, as explained by Woodsmoke, is: "A day hiker will look down, see an M&M and step on it, crushing it to little bits. A section hiker will look down, see an M&M and walk around it. A thru-hiker will look down, see the M&M, pick it up and eat it and be glad he didn't have to carry the calories." The wait staff at Relia's Garden at the NOC observes the hiker appetites on a daily basis. Hamburgers are popular, but hikers "order according to calories and sometimes a hamburger isn't a big enough meal. They go for the largest meal." Hikers, for their part, are thrilled to eat in a restaurant. Said one during dinner, "I didn't have to fix it. I didn't have to clean it up, and I don't have to sit on the ground to eat it."

Thru-hikers comfort and amuse themselves with phone calls home, after they've gotten past the competition for a phone. With so many hikers on the Trail, competition is fierce, as Gutsy found out in Hot Springs: She went out at 3 A.M. to find an unused phone.

With parents and spouses, there is reassurance: "Yeah, I'm fine. . . . Yeah I'm eating. . . . No, I'm OK. . . . Knees and feet are fine." Bloody Nose's parents put his dog up to the phone so he could hear his dog bark a little. There are also comments about the scenery, "Have you ever heard of mountain balds? I've walked across several. . . . They're big grassy areas and nobody really knows why they exist. . . . You should see them. . . . I went across one . . . Siler Bald . . . it was huge." If the support person is a parent, there is discussion about where to send the next mail drop. "I should be in Damascus in about 10 days."

Depending on who the support person is, the conversation often takes that inevitable turn, and hikers, aware that their lives are becoming increasingly different from the folks' back home, play it to the hilt, "No, it's easy. . . . I just dig a hole and hang onto a tree. . . . no, it's not hard . . . no, not really . . . it becomes second nature after awhile." Usually the call wraps up pretty fast after that. The thru-hiker, of course, is grinning to beat the band. This part of hiking, telling war stories to family and friends back home, is *fun*.

In fact, somewhere in North Carolina, the hiking starts to become fun, on some days at least, for some hikers. Said Bloody Nose "My Trail legs are really kicking in and they're starting to feel stronger and hiking is getting to be enjoyable, as is the camaraderie. The first part of the week was snowy and very cold, even for this Yankee, but the latter part of the week was just gorgeous. Everyone has been in good spirits the last five days, now that the warm weather has arrived. I'm in even better spirits after a big dinner at the Trailside Cafe."

All thru-hikers it seems lose both their faith in and their reliance on elevation maps and weather reports. In fact thru-hikers, by the time they've been on the Trail a month, are cursing both. "Never, never, never, ever trust a profile map," cautioned Woodsmoke. "I was looking at the map and saw I had to do three ups. Well, I walked and I walked and I did what I thought was three ups, but I still wasn't where I thought I would be. I've gotten to the point where I don't even look at the maps. If the trail goes up, I go up. If it goes down, I go down. It really doesn't matter what the map says." Tom (of Tom and Millie) said about the April weather forecasts out of Atlanta, "Ten percent chance of rain means 2–3 inches of snow and a cold-ass night." The weather is whatever the weather is, and the hikers, if they intend to reach Katahdin, must walk in it or through it, whatever it may be. Thru-hikers come to accept that weather and terrain are non-negotiable and quit trying to strike bargains with God.

On March 31, the group at Hawk Mountain, Georgia, listened to the weather forecasts that called for clearing skies. On April Fool's Day, they awoke to sleet and snow and cursed the National Weather Service. As another cold front barreled through the southeast, the winds roared so loud you'd swear that 18-wheelers were having a derby in the sky. For Wildhair, who had just left the comfort of Walasi-Yi Center, "it was the

Jester, Trigger, and Lady Bug stop for a breather.
Wayah Bald, North Carolina.

most miserable night on the Trail so far." In the Smokies, "howling wind and low temperatures" forced 19 hikers into a shelter built for 12, observed Download. "Boot, socks, everything was frozen. Hung clothing was frozen."

On April 2, hikers awoke to 30 degree temperatures and a wind-chill down to zero. Despite the cold, they were happy: This was the first day in the last seven that was sunny. How hard could that be? Mountaintop views could be enjoyed, and gear could dry out. Before long the day actually turned into something quite pleasant— dare it be called spring? Catfish and Lord Bacon came rolling down into Neels Gap, smiling and laughing about the downhill haul from Blood Mountain, "It may be downhill all the way, but it's the roughest downhill I've ever seen." Ice and muck made the path difficult to navigate, but what the heck? The sun was out and the birds were singing. Ladybug, Jester and Trigger, after picking their way through the ice on Wine Spring Bald, North Carolina, stopped to enjoy the views from Wayah Bald Fire Tower—and their first sighting of wildflowers, bluets, at the base of the stone retaining wall. Further up the Trail, Download and Nexmo, discouraged initially by the dirty, crowded shelters they found in the Smokies, found the resolve to keep going. Hikers just starting from Amicalola felt blessed. On April 3, the night truly sparkled as a beautiful half moon rose over the AT. For the next few days, the shade given by head-high rhododendron felt wonderful as a warm April sun shone through the leafless woods, and for a change made thru-hikers wonder if sunburn was among the many Trail delights.

Early season hikers may have been becoming Trail-hardened, but they weren't Trail-hardened enough. So Mother Nature obliged by beating up on them some more. So what if at lower elevations daffodils and azaleas were blooming and the trees greening up? That was just part of a world these people had left behind. In their world, up on the Trail, fog and drizzle and cold clung to the mountains like dirt to the edge of moleskin.

A group that tried to camp on Max Patch learned the hard way. Foxtrot, Blue Sky, Skywalk, Breakin' Wind, Pixie Mouse, Charlie Brown, and Reno each set up a tent on top of Max Patch, North Carolina, a huge southern Appalachian bald that was once home to a landing strip. During the night as a front barreled through, winds pushed upwards of 70 miles an hour, nearing hurricane strength. Some of the hikers packed up and left, going downhill to get out of the wind. The others who stayed had their tents twisted. The next morning, after they had survived the night, they laughed about their night on 'Death Row.'

On April 8, hikers in North Carolina found themselves slogging through significant snowfall again. Standing Indian Mountain had seven inches, Wesser Bald about five, the Smokies nearly a foot, and Hot Springs about an inch. Backdraft, Cold Finger, Navigator, and

Springtime hasn't arrived yet at Wayah Bald Fire Tower, North Carolina.

Attitude found themselves doing the Albert Mountain slip-n-slide in about a foot of snow. Cold, cutting winds kept Download and Nexmo from enjoying the magnificent view from Max Patch and they wondered "when spring hiking would begin." Lots of hikers were wearing frozen boots and swearing about it because the only way they knew to thaw them out was to put them on. Some hikers, Attitude, Navigator, and Cold Finger among them, warmed theirs up with their stoves. Gutsy became disoriented from the cold and hiked a section of the trail twice, making for a 24 mile day. A fellow hiker said that when she showed up at Fontana Dam, she had "that 1,000 yard stare of a battle-fatigued soldier." And it wasn't just the frozen boots and fatigue that was causing the hikers to swear. Clouds obscured the views so much that one hiker said, "When I get to the Jesuit hostel in Hot Springs, I'm going to go to confession before I do anything else. I've been cursing left and right up the muddy slopes and every time I pass a Smoky Mountain vista in the clouds."

The weather toyed with the hikers throughout the middle of April. In Hot Springs rain fell on March Hare, Godfather, Turtle, Turbo, Slider, Chameleon, Bronco, Download and Nexmo. On Cheoah Bald, Attitude, Navigator, and Cold Finger found that the rain and clouds obscured another sunset.

Yet another wave of hikers leaving Springer Mountain chugged up the mushy Trail. Again hikers were amazed at how hard hiking the Trail was. After hiking in on-again off-again rain to Springer Mountain, Trail Gimp was wondering if she would even make it to the shelter. "I really wanted to see the terminus plaque on my first day," remarked Trail Gimp, "but about 2:20 it started to rain. Downpour, thunder, lightning . . . it was agonizing." With such a welcome to the Trail, she began to think about calling it quits. "I cried right in the middle of the Trail . . . couldn't figure out why I was punishing myself like that. I felt really sorry for myself. But I eventually realized that to get anywhere, I'd have to move forward or die right there on the Trail."

Then, from April 19 to April 21, the hikers from southwestern Virginia to Springer Mountain were treated to a spectacular storm front. No way was spring going to creep in gently. Spring in 1996 had started out as a fist fight, and all indications were that it was going to stay that way. With this storm the hikers saw it all.

Sir Goober Peas and Aunt Jemima, in Virginia, struggled with both rain and snow, complicated by hunger that bordered on dangerous.

"It was the longest stretch early in the trip, and we had grossly under-estimated our food rations. . . . a meager meal of plain instant oatmeal didn't warm me up a whole lot and I was chilled all day.

"We soon came upon Dismal Creek valley and stopped to take pho-tos of the falls. I had a mere three granola bars for 1.5 days of hiking. Famished, and knowing that we had at least 10 more miles for the day, I gobbled down all three on the spot and barely felt satisfied. We were down to three pop-tarts apiece. After gulping them down, I looked for any other edible morsel and found the most detested item. In an effort to spice up the variety of our peanut butter-on-bread lunches, we had bought some corn tortillas.

Rain had started as Sir Goober Peas and AJ snarfed the peanut butter smeared tortillas, and then fueled by this "heinous but available" source of calories, they started pushing up Sugar Run Mountain. As they gained elevation, the rain turned to snow, their seventh so far. Although the views were breathtaking, the two hikers were locked in the immediate and oppressive cold. Finally they came to the road to Woodshole. "The sun was in its last few minutes on the horizon," noted Sir Goober Peas when the pair were greeted by Highpocket, a former thru-hiker turned care-taker. In that little kitchen, warmed by a wonderful wood stove and able to cook a meal, Sir Goober Peas and AJ thought Mrs. Tillie Wood, her home Woodshole, and Highpocket to be extraordinary.

Sprout, who was up on Big Bald, Tennessee, that day, had to run for her life. "I've always been told that, in a lightning storm, you should spread out, stay low and get out of wide open spaces, especially if it was at high elevation. "'How silly' I thought every time I heard this. I would never put myself in such a situation.'"

"Well, I did. We were on Big Bald, at 5,516 feet, one of the highest mountains around, in the middle of a huge thunder and lightning storm with incredible winds. It all began as we started up the mountain.

"After eating some scrumptious oatmeal raisin cookies from three Trail Angels out on their yearly ritual of bringing cheer to hikers, Twisted Sister and I decided to hang back as the storm crossed above us. We were so close it was incredible. It really did sound like someone was bowling up there and making some amazing strikes.

"We stood there for about three minutes before the hail and wind and rain whipping my body was too much to handle. I wasn't even wearing a rain shell because I figured I was already wet, my clothes were wet from sweating, so why get another piece of clothing wet? Yet another stupid move.

"The wind gusts were so strong that they practically blew me off the mountain, and they were turning my skin to a lovely red. I was literally running across Big Bald, and the adrenaline pumping made my pack feel as light as a feather.

"This bald was BIG, and just as I thought it was over, another section would come up. It kept going and going and we kept running and running and praying that we would not turn into another statistic. Finally we made it to the shelter."

A little bit further south Godfather, Turtle, Download and Nexmo were themselves reminded about "who controls the heavens." In the Smokies, hikers were first treated to lightning that seemed to crack the sky in half. Then hail the size of peanuts pummeled them. Cowardly Lion and Munchkin just barely hitched a ride into Gatlinburg, and Pokey nearly made it to Ice Water Spring Shelter before the hailstones fell.

Medusa, caught on Wayah Bald in North Carolina when the hail storm started, tried to run the last six miles to Cold Spring Shelter with her fellow hikers. "That's not very practical with a 40-pound pack. We got very wet, and Gore-Tex is full of it."

Down in Georgia, Waldo decided to exercise thru-hiker mind over matter. Dressed in nylon shorts and Capilene T-shirt, he shouted to the mountain gods, "This is rain?! This is NOTHING! Show me some real rain!" Once challenged, the mountain gods responded. Temperatures fell to the 50s, lightning danced in the sky, and Waldo found himself hiking and practicing sign language just to make sure that his fingers were still working. Hypothermia was a distinct possibility. Trail Gimp, who had finally broken down and bought some aluminum hiking poles to help ease the severe knee and foot pain she had developed, wondered if she had just bought a ticket to become a lightning rod. "A bolt went down about 50 feet in front of me. I flipped. I had two aluminum hiking poles, an aluminum pack frame, and aluminum tent poles. It was raining so hard that the Gore-Tex got soaked." At Tray Mountain, the hail storm drove 15 hikers into the shelter, and they ended up crawling in their bags, head to toe, shoulder to knee. Sven, one of the 15, commented that they resembled sardines and all they really needed was "some soybean oil and a pop-top can." The laughter cheered them all.

Ah! April in the Southern Appalachians! Here the hikers were, on the rooftop of the southeast, hungry, cold and wet, hurting, trying to pursue a dream, and unable to see much of anything except rising clouds or sinking clouds or angry clouds. In these mountains, the clouds would roll in and the greens and browns of the trees would disappear into a whitish, gray mist and all that could be heard was the crackling of squirrels running on the trees. But just as quickly the clouds might roll out and reveal the interlocking fingers of the high ground, complete with a blue sky and emerald green spruce trees and the shy appearance of spring down below. At least the fresh, bright green smell of red spruce was in the air to intoxicate the hikers.

Weather wasn't the only major impact on the hikers during April. Most of the hikers traversed the Smokies well enough, although many opted to yellow blaze—hitchhike—around the park. For some reason, the Smokies intimidated many of the hikers. Other hikers noted that it was the first stretch of really remote Trail with no road crossings.

There were no serious bear encounters, for the hikers at least, although Jarhead's water bottle told a different story. Jarhead was at Spence Field shelter and "going to go down to the Spring to get some water. About halfway there—I'm slow, I'm an old man and my knees were sore—I saw the bear. I turned around, hightailed it back to the shelter and told Youngblood and Runaway Ralph 'Boys, we got company.'

"The bear followed me back to the shelter, and started doing a bear-dance on the metal food boxes. Finally he got tired of that and looked like he had had enough when he discovered a plastic grocery bag with some left over food in it.

"Well, that made me mad. Whoever left that bag there was just encouraging the bear in his habits, which were getting in the way of my getting to that spring. Finally, though, that bear seemed to have enough and we thought it had wandered off.

"So Youngblood, Ralph and I started back to the spring. But the bear hadn't left, y'see. He had just gone over this little ridge. So when we saw him, we turned around and went back to the shelter.

"That was when my water bottle slipped out of my pocket. I had been carrying it in my pocket, y'see. Well, the bear hustled up there—he had found himself a groundscore—and just as carefully as you please took that Nalgene bottle in his teeth and eased over the ridge with it.

"A little while later, I decided to have one more try at that spring. When I went over the ridge, there was no bear to be found, but you should have seen what he did to that water bottle. I guess he got more Nalgene than he bargained for!"

Further up in Virginia, some hikers ran into vicious dogs in and around Moreland Gap shelter. Because of past problems in the area, hikers speculated that local people were setting them up for dog attacks by advertising a side trail to a store.

Were it not for the Trail Angels who came to road crossings and shelters to spread a little cheer and good will, the 1996 thru-hikers might have felt a lot less optimistic about their chances of one day reaching Katahdin. Mark Lenyk from Dawsonville raised the spirits of many hikers when he appeared at Indian Grave Gap with bananas, apples, sodas, and homemade banana nut bread. Harvy "Hey, You Need A Ride," the unofficial but much appreciated and certainly celebrated Trail shuttler from Erwin, Tennessee, made life a little easier on Download, Nexmo, Godfather and Turtle in getting their mail drops from the post office in Erwin. Gutsy's day was brightened when Harry from the Greeneville hiking club treated her to a birthday dinner. Midnight and Out of Africa, who left Springer in early April, enjoyed the Easter dinner (turkey and trimmings) served to them at Goose Creek Cabins. Jeff, Megan, and Waldo had high praise for Gordo's Third Annual Addis Gap Feast, a brunch consisting of scrambled eggs, fried

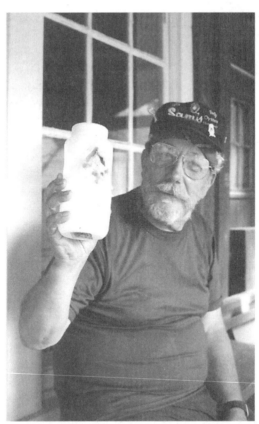

Jarhead and the Nalgene bottle the bear worked over.

potatoes and mushrooms, fruits and orange juice. As many as 80 hikers showed up for the sixth annual Rat Patrol party at Brown's Gap. The Rat Patrol, a group composed of thru-hikers from previous years, treated hikers to a fish fry on Friday night and a bar-be-que on Saturday. All the trimmings were available, along with homemade brews and sarsaparilla. (The homemade brew was some powerful stuff. After just one glass, Woody Pop knew he needed to hold right there.) They also served up breakfast, complete with bacon and eggs, the next morning.

It wasn't only people bearing gifts of food that earned the hikers' praise. Everybody who met Trail Angel Sam Waddle spoke of his good-natured outlook and of the good job he does. Gary Poteat and his wife Lennie at the Blueberry Patch earned points as the most hospitable Trail hosts. And certainly the hikers noticed and appreciated the work done by the Nantahala and Smoky Mountain hiking clubs: After Opal had come through, an average of 60 trees per mile were reported down. Now the Trail was clear due to their efforts and hikers were able to pursue their dream.

White Pine, a '95 thru-hiker, brought forth a lot of smiles at Newfound Gap with his fresh fruit and beverage stand. The hikers really appreciated his effort because Newfound Gap, the hikers discover, is a scary place. It's a cacophony of tour busses, school busses, sports utility vehicles and land yacht cars and little economy numbers. Cars are backing up, cars are turning in, and cars are squealing brakes as drivers joust for a good parking space. Tourists of all ages, shapes, and sizes mill around the stone edifice where Franklin D. Roosevelt delivered the commemorative speech for Great Smoky Mountain National Park. Children run about and try to hit each other and adolescent girls pull their sleeve cuffs over their hands to stay warm. The likelihood of being injured at the Trail crossover at Newfound Gap is high because very few people are watching for thru-hikers.

After spending about a month on the Trail and about four to five days in the Smokies, some hikers are stunned by the noise and the crowds, and they are flattered by the photo ops they have with tourists and some of the thru-hikers puff up a little bit as people ask them what they're doing. "Look, there's a real hiker," heard Nexmo. Whereas Neels Gap with its road noise and small hubbub of tourists is comforting, Newfound Gap is bewildering. It's especially so since, as Sir Goober Peas described it, "the typical Smoky Mountain experience for thru-hikers includes crowds at fenced-in shelters, lots of spring break and weekend troopers, all the garbage that these people leave, and park bears." Hikers who hitch into Gatlinburg generally come away feeling that the town and its crowded hubbub are a travesty. The hikers have become more at ease in the wilderness with Nature's sounds than they are now with the noise of tourist areas. Up in Blacksburg, Virginia, Heyokay sat in Gillie's trying to listen to a friend's conversation, but his "eyes kept darting out the window every time a person walked by. Walking outside I was more taken with the fact that dozens of people were scurrying about instead of anticipating the first bloom of spring."

In addition to being more at ease with nature after six or so weeks on the Trail, thru-hikers begin to feel a sense of community as they exchange their own kindnesses with each other. Little Bear, Cap'n Cool, Sun Spirit, Noodle, 9 Lives, Annapurna, Johnny Quest, and Goatherder appreciated John Allen leaving his mail drop behind for them to enjoy when medical reasons caused him to stop. Maple Leaf cheered hikers Bird, Big Dipper, Bearfoot, Allgood, Stinky, Download and Nexmo in early April with guitar music around a campfire. When Walkie-Talkie had to be evacuated from Roan Mountain due to a mysterious and life-threatening sickness, Allgood told him, "Man if you can just walk to the clearing where the helicopter is, I'll carry your pack." Allgood stood still for a moment while Walkie reached out and put a tentative, weak hand on Allgood's shoulder for support. Together they hobbled out to meet the helicopter. "Roan Mountain," Allgood noted, "seemed to be where mayhem happened."

After helping a mother with two children, the aptly named Yogi came back to the shelter to share the cookies and funnel cakes the mother had given her. A hiker passed along to Woodsmoke the tip that just a tiny bit of dish soap rubbed onto glasses kept the lenses from fogging. Annapurna, looking out for hikers everywhere, advised that "if you have long hair, remember to tie it back when operating your stove. I've burned mine twice now." Trail Gimp laughed at how everybody was handing out moleskin to hikers coming into the shelter. "It's amazing how generous strangers are. But I guess we're not strangers after sleeping with the same group of six to eight people for three nights in a row." At the Fontana Hilton, Pilgrim shared some rubbing alcohol with Early Mon and showed him how it cooled the feet and kept athlete's foot at bay. They shared a good laugh reflecting about how during the day, they'd be pushing up a hill and cursing every step when no one was around to hear them. "But" they laughed, "when you come into camp you just smile and say to everyone, 'Oh . . . great day. Great day. Easy hike. Easy hike.'" Several thru-hikers, including Zamboni Tow-Step, Dancing Bear, Screamin Knees, Cajun C and Gutsy had an impromptu cookout in the park in Damascus, Virginia.

Buzz pondered these amazing friendships and mused that "I don't think friendships like this are found in the 'regular world.'" Trail Gimp noted it too, saying, "It's really strange how Trail friendships quickly turn into Trail families." Skye echoed that sentiment, remarking that "nothing could prepare me for the reality of close-to-hypothermia encounters and the pain and despair in the faces of thru-hikers as they methodically pumped their stoves to get something hot into their bodies. The snow and nights below freezing were a very tough part for the beginning of the Trail. Nights in a shelter meant for 12, but housing 26 makes for incredible bonds, especially knowing that we have to help one another get through this. We might have started out as strangers, but we're like brothers and sisters now."

Landshark noted that "it's amazing all the stuff we humans take for granted: a warm night's sleep, running water, bills." Bull Moose, speculating on the spiritual pull of the trail, mused, "There are feelings I experience out here; call them primal, dream-like, spiritual, whatever. They are difficult to explain on society's terms. I do not know if the catalyst is walking, proximity, solitude, weather, friendship or deprivation. I just know I feel I'm a part of the earth and the earth is a part of me."

Despite the highs, there were the inevitable lows. Lobo's Pet had to hang out at the Fontana Hilton for a few extra days because his sister, thinking she was doing him a favor, sent his mail drop third class. The result was that when Lobo's Pet arrived at the post office in Fontana, his package hadn't. So running out of food, he did his best to endure the glitch. Screamin Knees, an ex-city cop, was on the Trail to escape a little of the stress that his job had put on him. "One of the draws for doing this was to get out of the city and away from the problems that are associated with an urban setting," he explained. Unfortunately, his escape couldn't be total. "We had pre-packaged mail drops and left them with my parents to send out. Cajun C's [his hiking partner], were coming to see us in Hot Springs, so they were going to physically bring the packages with them. While C's brother had the packages, someone stole them. Food was not the problem, it was just a financial loss. However, the mail drops contained several irreplaceable items such as letters from an entire fifth grade class. My niece was tracking our progress." Yoda became separated from her hiking partners ET and Turtle and spent a fearful night in the woods huddled under the trees. The EMS Crew #2 in Carter County, Tennessee, quickly assembled a search and rescue team. By 9 A.M. the good news was that Yoda had been found alive. She was tired, but safe. Trail Gimp, struggling with bloody, blistered feet, watched as her Trail friends left her behind. "I can see why some people would drop out due to loneliness. You need the people to keep you going."

Many hikers fell ill with some sort of virus that was lurking between Davenport Gap and Hot Springs. Wingfoot, an esteemed thru-hiker living in Hot Springs served as Trail Dad, questioning hikers to see if the cause could be identified. Was it airborne? Was it something in the water? As he looked in and clucked over sick hikers at the Jesuit hostel—and autographed their copies of the *Thru-hiker Handbook,* a reference book that some hikers carry—Wingfoot took their good wishes to him in stride. "Wish yourselves good luck, because you're going to need it." Wingfoot's face wore the wry expression of someone who knew what he was talking about. Having thru-hiked the Trail 10 times before, Wingfoot knew exactly what kinds of challenges—physical, mental, and emotional—would continue to arise for the thru-hikers. Making it to Hot Springs was no guarantee of anything on the Trail, except of making it to Hot Springs.

For some hikers, the low spot was seeing just how many people come out to attempt a thru-hike. "Too many people out here." Other repeat hikers agreed, especially when they saw the wear and tear on the Trail. Bad Trail etiquette also angered some. Woodsmoke became angry with a day-hiking woman who allowed her dogs to urinate entirely too close to a spring. "They don't understand. That's the only water we might be able to find. They have cokes back in their cars, but that's our water." Allgood had an even worse experience. Stepping over a hill beyond a shelter on his way to the spring, Allgood stepped in what he realized was human feces. "It would be nice if we'd had some privies," he said, shaking his head in disbelief. Cajun C expressed her anger that she was having to pack out other people's trash. "Here I am with 40 pounds on my back, and picking up and carrying other people's litter."

Kick-a-Tree laughed about a personal low he had at Simp Gap, North Carolina. "It was a lousy afternoon, rain and hail. I was standing in the parking lot and thinking about the next climb into Stecoah Gap. A Jeep Cherokee rolls into the lot and a lady rolls down her tinted window and hollers in a squeaky voice, 'hey, I want to take your picture . . . you look so pathetic!' She does her deed, rolls up her window, and drives off. I thought lightning and hailstorms were my low point. But I was wrong. She didn't even toss me a Snickers bar."

m a y

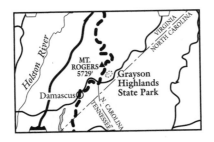

AH, YES, THE WORLD IS GREEN.

-Bloody Nose

In a wild symphony of green, May started arriving on the Appalachian Trail. It crept up the mountains, and for a very long time the trees looked as if they had been dipped, ever so slightly, in yellow-green paint. But eventually, even at the highest elevations, hikers began to see the rusty red green of budding maples, and the low green of blackberry brambles, and the yellow green of the poplars, and the pea green of the wild cherry trees.

Against the emerald green of rhododendrons and pines appeared the greenish-white of the dogwoods, the tiny white of wild strawberry blossoms, and the dusty white of dandelion seeds. Violets and purple trillium carpeted the ground in moist areas, and here and there the branches of red bud trees lilted with tiny, fuschia-colored flowers. Patches of bluets covered the rolling Virginia meadows, and hikers breathed air perfumed with lily-of-the valley. Flame azaleas in yellow and orange and peach zig-zagged on the mountain sides. Leaves in hundreds of shapes—round and low, spikey like blades, shaped like palms or hearts, or pointy like needles— were born. With the new leaves came the sound of fluttering breezes. No longer draped in splotches of gray and brown, with trees creaking in the cold winter winds as if they were about to snap apart, the world exulted in its rebirth.

Hundreds of hikers were on the Trail, and the human bracelet stretched from Virginia to Georgia. Hikers who were just leaving Amicalola in early May saw a far different Georgia than the ones who left in March.

"Thunder was in the background all day, and it finally decided to give us a shower in the afternoon. But the flowers are beautiful. I've taken plant taxonomy and am carrying a flower guide, so this is neat," noted Sneakers. Hikers who saw nothing but snow and ice in March probably wouldn't believe that flowers grow in Georgia, too, but late season hikers knew it to be true. A week or so away from Shenandoah National Park in Virginia, Zuma confided that "although there were a few days in the Sno-kies when I could get no sleep because I was trying to stay warm, now that the leaves are coming out, we are beginning to see a softer, friendlier side to the Trail." Painting a magnificent picture of a mid-spring, clear air sunset, Waldo described the moment at Cheoah Bald, North Carolina: "It began with the sun turning that light orange, outlining the clouds in front of it. Then it dipped lower, shading the trees and giving all of the mountain folds an amazing level of depth, lighting the clouds from within. Then the sun's edge touched the earth, turning it blood red and lighting the clouds from beneath, giving their tops an ominous dark shadow. From there the sun seemed to be sucked down, disappearing in seconds leaving us in twilight."

Elsewhere, people hurried to and from their jobs, their errands, their daily routines and watched spring arrive in their asphalt and clock-governed lives with only passing notice. Not so for the Appalachian Trail thru-hikers. They were living this change of seasons, living it with every step they took.

The challenges, of course, weren't over, even as the weather moderated. Steve and Lea found Siler Bald shelter "full" and together with other thru-hikers had to tent through a wild thunderstorm. Overcrowding, still a problem in the Smokies, caused thru-hikers to compete for bunk space in the shelters, where they continued to be amused by novice hikers. One night as they slept once again in a crowded shelter in the Smokies, the sound of a father thrashing his backpack with his walking stick awakened Bonnie and Clyde.

Hwoooff! exploded the sound across the shelter.

"Daddy, Daddy, look at the mice. Look at the mice!"

Hwoooff! came the sound again.

"Get him, Daddy get him!"

Hwooofff!

"Get him, Daddy, oh get him get him!"

"Do you have food in your pack?" Clyde questioned through the darkness.

"Yeah."

"You shouldn't have food in your pack. Do you have food in your sleeping bag?"

"Yeah."

"You shouldn't have food in your sleeping bag, either."

"Well, are they going to run around all night long in here?"

"Yeah. You'll never get any sleep if you don't learn to ignore shelter mice."

Other hikers had trouble understanding why their fellow hikers tolerated the mice. "I hate mice," stated Betty Crocker, "and I can't figure out why these hippies are against mouse traps, while not one says anything against shooting boars." Lucky (?) for the hikers, the mouse problem seemed to lessen as the temperatures warmed up and the snakes came out.

Not that May was all flowers and leaves and grass and sunshine. It wasn't. Trail Gimp welcomed the month by looking outside her tent to see a romantic, near-full moon shining directly into her tent. But, she went on to note, "it was light enough to see shadows of mice crawling all over my tent, under the rainfly, trying to get in. I wasn't particularly scared, just a bit irritated." Annapurna gambled and lost with the rain. "As I crossed Fontana Dam the rain began to sprinkle on [Dragonfly and me] and by the time we stepped into the woods, it just opened up." Annapurna pulled her way up the steep Shuckstack mountain haul anyway. What was her choice? "We made it to that first shelter, Birch Spring, which is a dump of a shelter, and called it a day."

The month was by turns hot and cold, wet and dry. On May 4 at Knot Maul Branch shelter, Gutsy just put out her Therm-a-Rest on a ground cloth and slept underneath her sleeping bag, underneath the stars and a big, round moon. On the 6th, Download was pitching his tent in the rain—again.

On the 8th the weather was once again hot enough for some old-fashioned river fun. Trail Gimp, who was hanging out in Hot Springs trying to let her bum ankle heal, went with a group of 11 other hikers to the railroad trestle in order to go diving into the French Broad River. With everybody soaked and laughing, it wasn't long before the Thru-Hikers

Leaving Hot Springs, North Carolina.

Co-ed Naked Bridge Jumping Team was born. "Nine hikers, men and women, of all different body shapes and sizes, dropped drawers and threw shirts, and climbed up to the railroad tracks and started walking across the tracks to the middle of the river. 'Where are you supposed to look?' I wondered. You try to keep eye contact, but how can you look someone straight in the eye, try to remain serious, when you're outside and they're buck naked? Anyway, they all jumped and I served as the designated photographer." Trail Gimp also served as the designated spokesperson when the local cop appeared on top of the railroad tracks, too.

But then on May 13, Think About It walked through snow on Chestnut Knob. Seeing snow on the mountain tops, hikers wondered how much of what they saw was snowflakes and how much was petals dropping from the trees. In the Smokies Bonnie and Clyde hiked through rain and snow and fog and saw nothing of the views. Then on the 14th temperatures rose into the 70s and for the first time in the season, thru-hikers found themselves struggling with the heat. Sweet Dreams didn't care for the change at all. "The weather was too humid, too hot. When you walk with 60 pounds on your back and you climb straight up for more than seven miles, that's hard."

Once again high up on the mountaintops, with the days punctuated with monster thunder and hail storms, hikers often found themselves running, as did Scamper and Rosy. "I enjoy being a spectator in the stadium of the sky, but as my wife and I were on the AT starting another enjoyable day, the weather to the west got darker as we proceeded. I watched it to see what it might do for as long as I could. But we dropped down into a ravine and stopped at a spring for water.

"The sky we could see was breaking up, so we took a break, which was a mistake. As we climbed out of the ravine and onto the crest of the ridge, I looked over my shoulder and there was a black wall. We took off to the next shelter.

"We weren't but half a mile from the shelter when the rain came down in buckets and then the lightning. I love lightning when I'm a spectator, but when we hit the top of the hill, we became players in the game.

"Bolts of lightning struck everywhere, and then one flashed past us within meters. We broke into a trot down the muddy trail. But not 10 meters down the trail we smelled smoke from the strike. It was a hair-raising experience, literally, beautiful but deadly."

As much as the weather and the terrain do matter to thru-hikers, both become only the canvas upon which the hikers forge their Trail bonds and begin to discover a deeper understanding of themselves.

Way up at the Mount Rogers Visitor Center in Virginia, Download and Nexmo spent a night on the porch with Chameleon, October Dawn, and Lobo's Pet. After a nearby Pizza Hut delivered the goods, the group enjoyed clear skies and a full moon. "Roughing it?" asked Download about this serene and wonderful evening with this evening's camping partners. "Not really." In Elk Park, Sweet Dreams credited her stay on the Trail to the support from fellow hikers. "I've been on the Trail five weeks already, and now I'm able to hike more than I was the first week. After three weeks, you really see a difference, but more important than that are the new friends on the Trail. Without them, I'm sure I would have been home by now." At the Fontana Hilton, Edsel found empathy and comfort from his hiking friends. "I thought at first I was the only person out here having problems, but soon I discovered that nobody is hiking pain free, no matter how well they appear to be. But other than a pair of sore knees, this hiking thing is great. There is much more of a roving community than I ever expected. I have yet to meet an unfriendly hiker."

And what about an unfriendly Trail town? There may certainly be some—rumors of dog attacks near Moreland Gap shelter indicated that such communities exist—but in the colorful month of May, the focus for many thru-hikers, as well as past thru-hikers, is a little town called Damascus, in Virginia, known as the "friendliest town on the Trail." In 1996 Damascus went all out to express its affection during its annual Trail Days, a week long celebration.

Damascus is one of those wonderful, front-porch towns that is unabashedly friendly, like a puppy that loves you because you're there. Other trail towns may also be friendly, but Damascus loves the thru-hikers. Even townspeople who have moved away come back for Trail Days. One former resident, whose home used to be the "scale house," talked about her years spent watching the thru-hikers. "I've seen so many hikers, I just love to come back and see 'em again. They're so much fun. Oh, I reckon there's a lot of drinkin' and sex over there in the tents. But that's evrawhere, don't you think?"

That Damascus is special is obvious at first glance. The Appalachian Trail comes into town by a long finger of a park, turns a sharp right at an old steam engine, crosses a concrete bridge and goes right through the center of town. Trees line Laurel Avenue, the main street, and people still sit in swings on the front porches of white clapboard bungalows and wave to each other. For the hikers, the town put out green flags with the familiar white blaze to point the way through. Red, white, and blue bows decorated most telephone poles, and red geraniums, orange poppies, and pink begonias adorned many front porch steps. This little town, tucked in the mountains of Virginia, provides a visual feast to celebrate the thru-hikers' arrival.

Before the festivities began, hikers hung out at either Mt. Roger's Outfitters (MRO) or The Place, talking about their gear, buying new gear, looking for others who might have gone ahead, or checking out the Trail register. Problems with water filters seemed rampant, a situation that Damascus Dave, thru-hiker owner of MRO, attributed to a combination of improper maintenance and hikers trying to filter water directly from mud holes. It was an echo of an assessment Jeff Hansen had made earlier about the hikers as they passed through Neels Gap: simply *having* top-notch gear wasn't enough. A hiker had to know *how* to use it. Otherwise the stresses of the Trail would break the gear, just like it would break the hiker.

Word went out that Kraft was giving away boxes of mac and cheese, four to a hiker, so hikers shuffled over to MRO for more of their favorite Trail haute cuisine. Imagine: tuna mac was in their futures! The town laundry did a brisk business and hikers draped themselves around the pay phones. As Navigator explained it, "Trail towns are awesome. You get to eat—all you can, you get to sleep—on sheets, sometimes—you get to take a shower. And you get to wash that shirt you have been wearing for the past five days. Best of all, you can call home and talk to the folks." Early in the week the excitement built and it looked like this was going to be the best Trail Days in recent history.

Coming into town for Trail Days. Damascus, Virginia.

However, Trail Days started going wrong in a big way early on Tuesday, May 14. That night, hikers staying at The Place, a hostel supported by the Damascus United Methodist Church, were called together for a joint meeting held by Elizabeth McKee, mayor of Damascus and the local sheriff. Inmate #767971202 had escaped from the Northeastern Tennessee Correctional Facility and was still at large. His partner had been captured, but #767971202 was not to be found.

Officials described this guy as one bad actor. Serving a life sentence for murdering a 75 year old woman, #767971202, along with his partner, had escaped in a garbage bin. He was easily recognizable by a knife scar over his left eye, and hikers were warned not to hike alone, and preferably to avoid the Trail altogether. For a short while, seven miles of the Trail were closed and another 20 miles were under surveillance.

Hikers close to the prison heard the warning siren go off and at first thought it was a noon-day whistle. However, after checking watches, they suspected that it had to be something else. Soon, officials were on the Trail with dogs, helicopters were in the sky, and some hikers were being questioned and escorted away as they came out of the woods to cross US 421 and Tennessee 91, thus keeping them from hiking into town.

Many of the hikers were frightened by this turn in events mainly because they carried on their backs everything an escapee would need: a change of clothes that would double as a disguise and food.

The Golden Kiwis, a hiking couple from New Zealand who had the year before decided to take two and a half years after beginning their retirement to wander the world as "geriatric gypsies," realized how vulnerable they would be at night when they had taken out their hearing aids. If the escapee chose them as a target, they'd never hear him approach. Catfish felt queasy when he crossed the road to re-enter the woods and an official carrying a shotgun told him that the escapee was "about his size." He decided to hike with his pocket knife within easy reach. The thick cover of the rhododendrons that had once been friendly seemed like a perfect hiding place. For Sweet Dreams, knowing she was out in the woods with an escaped convicted murderer caused a weird feeling that she didn't like. "I thought many times about what would happen if I met him." Of course some hikers masked their concern with bravado. Woody Pop thought about it for a moment and said, "I'd find a way to get his gun and make him carry my pack."

For another New Zealander, also called Kiwi, the whole event provided some interesting Trail Magic, the thru-hiker name for the unexpected good things that happen on the Trail. Kiwi was coming out of the woods to cross a highway and was rather taken aback when he saw an armed law enforcement officer. "I was told that this person was armed and definitely dangerous and that he was serving a life sentence for murder. I was also rather fascinated with how this officer seemed to be armed to the teeth. (Police officers in New Zealand are not normally permitted to be armed and handguns are totally illegal.) I was allowed to continue after I was given advice on how to react if I came across this man. Apparently the escapee had been out in the mountains for several days and would undoubtedly be hungry and looking for food.

"I crossed towards Damascus and hiked, taking care to be aware of any movements in the undergrowth. After about three miles I was stopped by another office from the Tennessee facility, who told me that the Trail was about to be closed while the search continued, that I must return to the highway and that I would be escorted.

"We were soon joined by two more officers and their bloodhounds, as well as three other thru-hikers. It was rather a surprise to me that two of the other hikers were also from New Zealand, the Golden Kiwis. We had not met before, and apart from the urgency of the situation, I rather enjoyed talking with others from my own country, indulging in our own specific and different accents. I had been finding many of the American accents very difficult and it was something of a pleasure that for once I was actually able to understand all that each of us were saying to each other. To the best of my knowledge, we were the only three New Zealanders undertaking thru-hikes during this year."

More Trail Magic happened when local residents, recognizing that you couldn't very well hold a Trail Days without hikers, drove to places where the Trail had been closed in order to give hikers a hitch into town.

Meanwhile, hikers poured into town. Hikers who had already passed through hitched rides back and thru-hikers from years past were coming in for a reunion with their hiking friends. Over by the river, Tent City grew by the hour, as did the number of tents pitched outside of The Place. Former thru-hikers wandered over to The Place, doling out encouragement. "Ah! I love the smell of thru-hikers," exclaimed one as he passed several newly-arrived hikers. "Don't ever take a shower, don't ever wash your socks, don't ever wash your underwear," he directed them as he disappeared up the stairs. Coming back down the stairs, he smiled, leaned over to one of them again and sniffed audibly, "Just wanted one more hit of that thru-hiker smell!"

The town had organized quite a schedule of events for the three days. Master storytellers spun their yarns, the PTA pitched a fine spaghetti dinner, the Damascus Volunteer Rescue Squad served up two sausage and egg breakfasts, the Damascus Senior Citizens hosted a bean dinner, Warren Doyle an eight-time AT hiker entertained with his trail stories, the Damascus Methodist Church sponsored a pancake breakfast, and the Damascus Volunteer Fire Department Auxiliary topped it off with a chicken bar-be-que. Down by the river, hikers competed in the trout rodeo ("How do you hold on?" they asked each other.). Over in the park, hikers could enter their dogs in the dog show ("the first step to the Westminster Dog Show," laughed Pirate), race rubber duckies, enter the cakewalk, or get a T-shirt printed with "Hold For AT Hiker" and a special Damascus postmark. Over in the Methodist Church itself, videos and talks were given about how to stick to the thru-hike (Sluggo was hero of the day when he coaxed a VCR into working), the joys of hiking the Trail, and of other trails that hikers might want to hike another day. The biggest events of all, though, were the hiker parade and the hiker talent show.

In a town redolent with the smoky aroma of bar-be-que chicken, the town's police car and a Virginia State Highway Patrol car led the parade, lights flashing and sirens whooping. Following behind rolled the town ambulance, lights flashing too. Even the humidity could not dim the spectacle. Close behind the flashing lights walked the boy scouts. Miss Appalachian Trail rode in the back of a pickup and waved bravely at the admiring crowd. Next came the marching band, and finally the hikers, walking along in the standard hiker uniform: Tevas or boots, supplex shorts, Capilene shirts and OR hats or ball caps. One or two sported full pack regalia. At the Methodist Church hikers instigated a little water balloon and soaker hose war with past hikers, but given the heat, the splash of water felt great.

As hikers gathered for the talent show, some entered the cakewalk, a fund-raiser for the Damascus Little League. Heck, for the twenty-five cents entry fee, they might win a cake. After a few rounds, Catfish won a cake. A few rounds later, Tank won some brownies. Both were good naturedly hassled about whether they would share their winnings with their fellow hikers.

Later the talent show started. Twenty three hikers performed for the crowd, and the acts ranged from the mildly questionable to the strange to the pretty darned good. John the Baptist's rendering of Rindercella warmed up the crowd nicely, and many hikers were impressed with Beorn's recitation of Romeo's soliloquy at Juliet's window. CrossStone had the group going when he attempted for the first time ever to juggle four open and full soda cups. (The world still awaits the perfection of this stunt . . .) With a smile Morning Glory sang "Instant Breakfast," and Little Turtle sang a capella an almost bluesy, slightly modified rendition of "Lean on Me": *sometimes on our hikes,/ we all have pain,/ we all have sorrow* . . . Annie and the Salesman performed a vaudeville-like number and MacGuyver juggled. Waldo juggled torches and looked plaintively at the crowd and said "Ouch," when he accidentally grabbed a smoking part of the torch. Hasul and Tree performed on their didgeridoos, making strange, primal, intriguing sounds. Iron Phil sang Hiker Blues and Trail Magic (" . . . and I wake up to mice in my boots and in my hair—I love it!") Heavy Breather and Breakin' Wind sang "Livin' it up in the Hotel Appalachia," to the tune of "Hotel California." Fanghorn performed with his devils sticks, pleasing everyone when he did so with a pack on his back (internal frame) and coasting on a

Annie and the Salesman perform at Trail Days.

skateboard. Lagger amazed everyone with his Jew's harp performance, and the Hiker Formerly Known as Prince delivered a great rendition of "867-5309." Since the panel contained a few thru-hikers, a couple of hikers offered pop-tarts in order to sway the judging.

While the judges decided upon the winners, hikers cut loose as the performers walked back to the stage and ad-libbed in a jam/dance session worthy of the Druids. When the winners were announced, Iron Phil won first prize, John the Baptist second, Hasul and Tree third, and Little Turtle fourth.

By Sunday—with 2,400 boxes of mac and cheese given away and thousands of pancakes and eggs served up—hikers were quite satisfied that whatever pent-up hiker energy they had had been spent in Damascus. Surely the all night drumming over in Tent City helped expend a little energy too. The only irony of the festival came from the hiker parade. As the marching band marched down the street, they played, of all things, *Eleanor Rigby*. These hikers, who some four to eight weeks earlier didn't know each other, were certainly anything but lonely.

If the first mail drop along the Trail represents progress, then Damascus is where a first metamorphosis becomes obvious. So much has happened to the hikers, physically and otherwise, that by the time they reach Damascus fundamental changes are apparent in each person.

Some of the changes are physically obvious. Men are slimmer, and the women have more muscular legs. Bear was losing the padding around his collar bones and was concerned about his pack rubbing him raw. The letters AYCE (all you can eat) take on real meaning. "There's a big difference between a five day food supply at the beginning of the Trail and five day supply now," remarked Medicine Woman. "I used to eat two Lipton dinners every night in the beginning and I was never really full. Now I walk with a pound of squeeze butter and just pour it on my dinner. It works, and now I don't have to eat but one dinner." Rogue Bear bemoaned the fact that even his Lycra bicycle shorts were loose. "But," he grinned, "I now have a set of calves. I never had calves before." BB and the Purple Pirate were astounded by their appetites, "I never knew it was possible to eat this much! We had lunch twice yesterday and dinner all evening. We still have a watermelon for breakfast, plus we're eyeing TK's for omelets and grits." For H, the appetite was burning white hot and Virginia became a walking food fest. "Catawba, Homeplace restaurant—AYCE; Troutville, Country Cookin'—AYCE; Weasies—AYCE pancakes—$2.50 all day. Food, food, food—it's a big part of the Trail." A newfound creativity with Trail meals blossoms, for a boring meal is a meal partially uneaten, and thru-hikers have to eat. A Quanee put some spunk into his mac and cheese dinners with lots of garlic powder and black pepper. Using Trail registers, Walk With Wong shared Zenwalker's recipe for Thai ramen noodles that Zenwalker got from Sisyphus The Happy. (Just combine two packages shrimp ramen noodles with sundried tomatoes, throw in a little garlic, lots of Tabasco, and one tablespoon peanut butter. Voila! Thai ramen noodles!)

Other changes result from the euphoria of thru-hikers meeting their personal challenges. Obe-1-Knobe, who had lost 40 pounds and had already trimmed his pack weight by 14 pounds, laughed about his first nighttime hiking experience. "All these other guys had done it, so I thought I'd give it a try. It was like looking through toilet paper tubes, I tell you." Progress seemed slow and arduous and finally he decided to stop. "When I woke up the next morning I was only 50 yards from Jerry Cabin." Landshark hiked a 40-miler into Damascus. "I got here about 11:30 after walking through three rainstorms. I hiked the last two hours with gradually dimming maglights. I would have kissed the ground when I got here, but I wasn't sure if I could get back up." SunSpirit experienced a personal high after having completed her 40-mile day into Damascus. "Yesterday was the first time that I truly challenged myself to the ultimate limit. I left at 4 A.M. and stopped at every shelter along the way to refuel. I arrived around eleven at night, after having survived three heavy rain storms. Because I was physically drained, the mental awareness began to sink in. Life is an adventure, if you make it an option. No denying it!" Asked about her future plans, she smiled an angelic smile and said, "I'm looking forward to a 60-mile day. After awhile, the pain is the pleasure!"

With the arrival of spring, hikers are more at ease with and better able to appreciate the wilderness and its inhabitants. Jarhead marveled at the vivid orange of a cave salamander he spotted. A Quanee looked up to see scarlet tanagers and pileated woodpeckers. Bungalow Bill and Contrary Mary decided that bluets hugging the ground were their favorite wild-flower. Steve, Brandy, and Lea saw a bear cub just before Chattahoochee Gap and then almost immediately stepped on a rattlesnake that was sunning itself. Johnny Quest became poetic talking about the sunset he saw on Big Bald. Rogue Bear was amazed how distinct the sound of a rattlesnake is. "Even with my headphones on, I knew immediately what it was." Gutsy became entranced with lady slippers. Everyone thought the Grayson Highland ponies, the wind blowing in their wild manes, were fun. Waldo, thinking he was at Oz, watched the morning sun catch "the intricate webs throughout the forest, connecting flowers by delicate strands, leaves like marionette strings."

Trail-spun, hiker humor emerges as the best entertainment. Wildhair, hiking long days and staying focused on the Trail, saw a tortoise trudging south. He thought about pointing him in "the right direction," but instead just patted him on the belly. "Maybe he started at Katahdin," he mused. Betty Crocker earned his Trail name after a disastrous attempt to cook bread on a stick over a campfire. Several hikers set up day hikers they met to ask Mr. Bean, who was behind them on the Trail, if he had lived his entire life in Maine. Mr. Bean, very much alive and hiking, would laugh back, "Not Yet!" The Buns of Steel gang amused themselves with talk about how at Katahdin they would be able to "crack an egg on their posteriors without making a big mess of the egg." At Rusty's Hard Time Hollow, H and his fellow hikers danced to the—owww!—voice of James Brown in the headlights of Rusty's pickup truck. Calvin of Calvin and Hobbes, pointed out that Rusty, with his very basic, subsistence living circumstances, takes great pride in showing hikers that it doesn't take a lot of stuff—especially electronic stuff, because Rusty has no electricity—to have a good time. A joke—what's the difference between a thru-hiker and a homeless person? (Gore-Tex)—made the rounds.

And true to its nature, the Trail provided a place for hikers to work through their private demons and losses. For Sneakers, it provided a sanctuary to mourn. While hiking on the Trail, he learned via a phone call home that one of his best friends had been killed in a car accident. "It was hard. I built a stone monument on top of Standing Indian Mountain and christened it Jon Walker Mountain. The AT has let me mourn in my own way, and now I feel at peace. He was a great guy."

As a group, hikers are not able to indulge in the things that separate and isolate people—walls, television, cars—and as a consequence they rediscover themselves and others. "It gets lonesome out here sometimes and the people are all you have," noted Catfish. Robohiker, having been separated from his earlier hiking partners, hiked 70 miles in 72 hours trying to catch Greyhound and Poohbear. "It's an interesting part of the Trail I didn't think I would fall into," he noted. SunSpirit talked about Landshark singing them to sleep, and how she thoroughly enjoyed it. One night at a shelter, the song finished and SunSpirit asked him to "sing some more, man." "It's the end of the song," came the reply through the darkness. "So sing it again." "How about I sing another song?" CrossStone continued to write little poems in the Trail registers to cheer his fellow hikers, most of whom he'd probably never see:

Blister Mania

Blisters may come
And blisters may go
But blisters will find ya
Wherever ya go.
One thing's for certain
And this you should know
Make sure that you treat them
And away they will go.

Medicine Woman was having a devil of a time trying to filter water. "I was pumping and pumping and it was so hard. Then this hiker came over and put silicon on the o-ring. It made me want to ask 'who was that masked man?'" Bronco and Puddin offered to fetch water for Download and Nexmo and adopted Download as a hiking partner for awhile when Nexmo had to leave the Trail. For Sweet Dreams, her time in Grayson Highlands was perfection: "Sunny day, cool temperatures. A new shelter, only three days old with a good swimming hole nearby. A good supper, a baseball game in front, a fire with many songs. A guitar and marshmallows. Stars in the sky, and many wonderful friendly hikers. A Perfect Day!"

Sometimes hikers debated the use and misuse of the Trail. Should use be limited? Was the land being damaged? Were too many hikers out here? Many hikers, Rogue Bear among them, were concerned that many casual hikers overlook the very real fact that the AT is fragile and the Trail suffers from a false popularity fueled by love-it-and-leave-it media attention. "The Trail cannot afford to be put through the torture of the hordes that come out to trample the flowers, litter the land, scar the shelters and signs, and defecate in the water." Other hikers generalized to all trails and woodland areas, pointing out that more wilderness was needed, not less, and that more education concerning leave-no-trace practices was needed, not less. "Just look at the overflowing garbage cans and trash-littered paths in parks come Sunday afternoons," they point out. "Just look at the clogged up AT," they say.

One of Waldo's experiences at Ice Water Spring Shelter underscored the misuse and abuse of the Trail many hikers witnessed. "Around 1:00 A.M., two teenagers came into camp. One carried an immense boombox, the other a Marlboro backpack. They attempted to light a fire outside, but satisfied themselves with simply getting stoned. Before long they tried to get into the shelter. For bear protection, we had used the chain to fasten shut the gate from the outside. This is not hard to remove for a human, but it's a horse of a different color for a trashed human.

"None of us were awake enough or willing enough to undo the fence for them, so they rattled it a bit. They stopped, and a few minutes later we heard a clattering from up on the roof. One of them had climbed on top. Before long we saw a pair of feet poke out of the fireplace—he'd come down the chimney.

"Santa opened the gate for the other guy and they got up on the top bunk to sleep, sans sleeping bags in the freezing shelter. Morons. Needless to say, they didn't sleep too well. They left around dawn, boombox and backpack in tow. Yeesh."

All of the changes are quite substantial from the utter and complete exhaustion hikers experienced some six to eight weeks before when all they wanted to do was crawl inside their sleeping bags and go to sleep, hoping they'd wake up the next morning. The unease they felt about living outside has likewise disappeared. The hikers are stronger, sturdier people for having endured the challenges. Said CrossStone, "I think I'll deal with things better now after the Trail. Out here you can't get angry or wait for someone to solve your problem. You just have to find a way to solve the problem yourself."

Along with these rediscoveries of the self and the awakenings of environmental responsibilities, comes a new distaste for some of the things they left behind. Many hikers no longer subscribe to the formula that 'number of dollars spent equals perceived fun.' And certainly a stash of PepsiStuf isn't the key to happiness. Sisyphus The Happy remarked that "after only a month on the Trail, we're laughing at the radio commercials advertising things you can buy. Sure buying things is fun. It smells new and it feels new, but I've learned it only lasts a little bit. It's amazing to see how many people define themselves by what they buy. We're more interested out here in the things you discover you don't need and don't have to buy." Taking a break in Gatlinburg, Waldo turned on MTV. "Whatever happened to the 'music' part of 'music television'? I hardly saw a thing, just Beavis and Butthead. I swear I could feel my IQ drop as that show droned. I switched to the Weather Channel."

Even repeating hikers were accumulating new perspectives. Pirate, out on the Trail for his sixth thru-hike, said, "it's always the same but it's always different. Some people go to the mall every week to find different things. Me, I come out here." Echoed Bull Moose, who was making his second attempt, "Six months every five years is not too much to pay for keeping my life in perspective . . . this time I know I'm not going to freeze, I know I'm not going to starve, I already know that the road crossing will be there. I don't hike for the views because I've seen the views. This time it's more intense and internal what I'm learning about myself."

Many of the changes arise from the Trail Magic that thru-hikers experience. For Medicine Woman, part of the Magic too was listening to the stories people told her as they gave her rides. One Appalachian woman told her of the times when, living on a farm, she hatched a duck egg by tucking it into her bra and keeping it warm there. Many of the hikers, Jarhead and Attitude among them, noted that Erwin, Tennessee, was particularly friendly. The Golden Kiwis noticed it too, telling the story of a "gentleman in a pickup who picked us up and took us to a motel. When we saw that it was full, he took us to another one and waited with us to make sure we'd have a place to stay." Waldo remembered that Jeff Hoch, manager of the Fontana Motel, filled up hikers' fuel tanks, gratis. "A Trail Angel if I've ever seen one."

For their part, many hikers repay the generosity they receive by passing it along to others, either on the Trail or off. Zamboni Tow-Step's parents helped Download, Ole Swamper and Grasshopper slackpack while they were visiting their son at Woodshole. Mr. Bean so thoroughly enjoyed his stay at Woodshole that he was glad to "do the dishes for Tillie." In late May when Nexmo returned, Download and she had the opportunity to "dispense a little Miller Lite Trail Magic" of their own with Northbound Zak,

Duffbuster, Bloody Nose and One-Armed Bandit at Bryant Ridge shelter. The next night, the same crew celebrated Download and Nexmo's wedding anniversary, with Puddin surprising them with a no-bake cheese cake. Bungalow Bill and Contrary Mary found two cairn terriers on the Trail, both with tags. Not recognizing the local phone numbers, they adopted the two dogs and resolved to keep up with them until the next town. "It was obvious that they were house dogs. Their pads weren't tough at all. Pretty soon both dogs found it difficult to keep up, so I had to carry one and Mary carried the other. When we finally got into town, we placed a collect call to the owner

Sisyphus the Happy picks up a mail drop in Damascus, Virginia.

in the name of the dogs. The woman was overjoyed that her pets had been found and returned to her." Waldo, upon seeing that some people who had just given him a ride had only Hefty bags for rain gear, gave up a pair of rain pants. "I figured I owed a little Trail Magic, what with all I'd gotten."

Generalizations don't explain who the hikers are and why they hike, and throughout the month, hikers were disturbed by an article in *Outside* magazine that generalized about them, using information gathered from a very few. So incensed were they that a copy of the article floated among the shelters, with hikers reading it and threatening to cancel their subscriptions. "My catalyst, journey, and destination are nobody's business but mine," stated Bull Moose flatly.

Contrary to often-held misconceptions, the majority of hikers aren't social misfits, unable to fit in anywhere else in the world. Far from it. While they may hold uncommon opinions, they could, in fact, be anybody and often are. They might be young, they might be retirees. They might be male, they might be female. They might be liberal in their political views, they might be conservative. They might not hold any political views at all. They might have served in the military, or they might ridicule the military. They might be sophisticated or they might be rude. They might be working professionals or they might never have held a job. They might be doctors, lawyers, puppeteers or musicians or bums. In short, they form a cavalcade of humanity in lug-soled boots.

After several weeks on the Trail, however, one thing does begin to characterize them: It is a sense of *belonging* to a world where different, and arguably more important, things matter. The Appalachian Trail is both one of those things that matter and a powerful symbol of that world. Jester, a '94 thru-hiker introducing Warren Doyle, one of the Trail's legendary thru-hikers, for a talk during the '96 Trail Days, illustrated it perfectly, saying ". . . here's Warren Doyle who loves our trail as much if not more than anybody." *Our* Trail.

The sense that they belong to this different world and that with the Trail they belong to a community of hikers is born in the crowded shelters, the frosty mornings, the sunsets, the delicate blossoms of spring flowers, and the storms they witness together. It is born in the determination to keep going, not admitting defeat. It is born, too, in the Trail Magic extended to them by people they don't even know and in the kindnesses they extend to each other.

By Damascus it comes of age. Which is good. Former '94 thru-hikers Bad DNA and Squirrel, looking at the exuberant hikers on the streets of Damascus and cutting their eyes up to the ridge that the Trail follows out of town, shook their heads with a knowing smile. "After Damascus," they agreed, "it only gets harder. The party's over."

It's hard to understand how the hiking can become harder. By Damascus, thru-hikers have covered 452 miles. What is there left to learn or adjust to? For the most part, winter weather and snow are behind the hikers unless Mother Nature does something freakish. The sawtooth terrain in Georgia and North Carolina has given way to the somewhat gentler, rolling, high meadows of Virginia. Mornings are cool and hikers, looking down into the valleys from their skyline path, can enjoy seeing the mist cover the valleys. Although afternoons might turn warm, leaves dance in the breeze and provide a hushed music. When the day cools again, the evening sky deepens into royal blue, turns inky and then reveals a heaven full of stars. During the day, hikers pass through blooming spiderwort in purple, blue, and pink and lush, waist-high ferns. They see wild turkeys and cave salamanders and birds of all kinds. From a distance, when they're lucky, they see bear cubs following Mom into the woods. The Big Dipper appears nightly overhead, and hikers so inclined can look into the velvet purple blackness of the sky and watch the Dipper—and a thousand other stars not obscured by city lights— spin 'round. How hard can it be?

The siren call of hanging out in Trail towns overwhelms some hikers, especially those who are injured. It makes sense to take some time off to heal, but as they take more and more days off, they fall further and further behind. It's hard to remember during the lucious month of May that miles have to be made and that thru-hiking is more than hanging out in Trail towns, regardless of how much fun that might be.

Injury seems to sneak up upon a hiker despite his or her best efforts to work through it. Eventually circumstances conspire to prompt a thru-hiker to quit, as Kick-a-Tree learned. "May 8th was as mixed up as one day could possibly get. My mind was swimming with thoughts of home and spending time with my family. Daydreaming was about the only thing that took my mind off of my knee and foot, which I injured on a downhill about two weeks earlier. It wasn't mending well and I kept getting slower.

"That night I camped near Frozen Knob, about five miles south of Hogback Ridge Shelter, and I was visited by what sounded like a young black bear and a hunting dog. It was bizarre!

"These critters droned on like a circling freight train for at least two hours. First the bear came through my camp at a full gallop, then the dog. It would get quiet . . . then the dog charged through, followed by the bear. I got no sleep and wondered if this was some sort of conflict dream. The next morning after hiking, though, I came upon a quarter mile stretch of trail that had no less than five deposits of two types of dung. One looked very much like dog and the other . . . well I guess that was my bear!

"I finally reached Hogback Ridge Shelter and decided to hang out for the day. I needed to get my head clear and decide my next move. The one thing I didn't want to do was get off the Trail. I sat down, had some lunch and rested. A few hours passed, and some thru-hikers rumbled into camp, with a beagle trailing them. She had followed since the day before; they had given her water and food. Although she was tagged and had a phone number on her collar, they weren't planning on stopping to call. I said I'd take her in the next day.

"I started out to Sam's Gap on US 23. Before I reached the highway, I leashed the dog to keep her from traffic. On our way down, she tangled my legs with the leash and I came crashing down the hill. My bad leg was just about useless.

"I hobbled to a plant nursery and endured an intense tongue lashing about how I should have left the dog to fend for herself. The gentleman, however, took the dog, when he recognized the owner's name. I hobbled off to a diner, ordered two cheeseburgers all-the-way and drank a quart of Pepsi. Then I asked about a phone to get a taxi to Asheville, washed my bloody knee. The cabby took me to the bus depot and 24 hours later . . . I was home.

Hikers who are struggling to stay on the Trail contend with uninvited critiques of their lack of progress. One hiker, whom Trail Gimp met in Hot Springs, "tried to convince me that the only way to hike the AT was his way only. And he had to do at least 20 miles a day to get to Katahdin before October 15. He degraded anybody who skipped miles to get to Damascus for Trail Days, made fun of those who were hiking slow, told me to consider getting off the Trail and starting again next year to 'have a real thru-hike.' Even when I get to Maine and come back to do the miles I missed, he said it wouldn't be a real thru-hike 'because it wasn't done in order.'"

Hiking partners and hiking couples find that they have adjustment issues, oftentimes over hiking pace. "I started with one partner," said Medusa, "and we are still together, although he really annoys me because he is a speed hiker." Cajun C teased Screamin Knees, smiling and asking him, "What do you think this is? A race?" "We bicker mainly when we are low on food," said Lea about hiking with Steve. Couples realize that cooperation is a must because of the way they've decided who carries group items, such as tent and stove. "Besides," said Bonnie and Clyde, "you can't stay mad forever. Eventually you walk it off."

For some, the rewards are just too small. Thru-hikers must learn to content themselves with small rewards—a cold Pepsi at the gas station at the next road crossing, a letter from home, an extra day at Woodshole Hostel, or the cushioning that's restored to your socks after you've washed them.

Zuma summarized it perfectly. "It would seem at this point in the hike you have gotten over most of the frustrating aspects such as over-crowding of the Trail, familiarity with your gear and daily chores, how to deal with the elements, and just getting your body adjusted to the long miles. The only things that would stop someone now would be injury, boredom, or the desire to see loved ones back home. Long days of 20+ miles are routine and it is hard to cut back because you feel as if you are letting yourself down by doing even a 15 mile day. But you must try to be flexible or you might drive yourself insane and off the Trail." Wanderlust, an experienced hiker, emphasized Zuma's comment. "If you're putting in 20+ mile days and you hate it, stop. If you're putting in 20+ miles a day and have something left over for yourself at the end of the day, then you're fine."

But many hikers discover that they aren't fine at all. Fatigue, both mental and physical, begins to extract its price if injury hasn't. Hikers call it the 'Virginia Blues.'

Five hundred of the 2,158 AT miles are in Virginia, more than the three states the hikers have already hiked through just to get to Damascus. No state goes by more slowly for the hikers, and "nobody ever talks about how boring it is," remarked Tarkus, a thru-hiker in 1992.

A major component of the Virginia Blues is injury and "plain old physical exhaustion," Robohiker noted. Lucky hikers who initially dodged knee problems find themselves plagued with stress fractures in their feet. A Quanee knew about the constant physical pain: "Almost 600 miles and my feet are still a major source of pain. Blisters *under* calluses never seem to go away completely and hurt some days but don't hurt other days. Because my feet are experiencing a new pain, I'm taking more and more breaks. A good 10 minute break usually gets me two–three miles. While it's not severe, it is still a bummer. I literally tiptoed on my right foot for 30 to 40 percent of a 12 mile hike."

Gutsy limped into Harper's Ferry, not sure if she had a whopping case of tendonitis or stress fractures in her left leg. H, speaking of what May had been like for him, said, "May has also been a trying time on the Trail for me. After a sprained ankle at the start of the trip, everything was groovin' physically, meaning that I could do the miles if I wanted. In Damascus I was reunited with my buddy Asphalt and hiked with him to Pearisburg, where we came to a road. He looked at me and said 'I'm through' and started punching the ground. It was a bad scene. He gave me some batteries he didn't want, said he didn't want to talk about it. We shook hands and walked away. It was hard to take. He had been walking on torn ligaments in his ankle for many weeks. He had planned this hike for seven years. . . The ranks are getting smaller and it saddens me."

Roses, watching other hikers leave the Trail, noted that he had "seen many people burn themselves out by hiking long miles everyday." To get the most out of his hike, he "refused to go more than 20 miles a day" and as a spoof started a "Just Say No to 20s" program. "Although out here we all 'hike our own hike,' I try to get people to realize there's more to the Trail waiting to be discovered if you're only willing to take a few steps to the left or right."

Download hit a wall in Troutville because Nexmo had left the Trail due to a family emergency, "The scenery passed by without my noticing, and each step became a chore." Many hikers experience a loss similar to Download's when the partner they start with decides, for whatever reason, to leave the Trail. Hiking alone is not what they had in mind.

Sometimes it's not burnout, boredom, loneliness, or injury that hikers fall prey to: it's disease. Once the cold weather disappears, bugs of all varieties appear. Gearmaster found four ticks on himself while at Rusty's, pulled them off and didn't think anymore about it. A week or so later he developed Lyme disease and had to take three weeks off. Even when he got back on, hiking was difficult. "I struggled to get through Shenandoah. Normally I wouldn't care for the frequent road crossings and waysides, but in this case I was grateful to be able to take long breaks, rest, and try to eat real meals." For Gearmaster, suffering with Lyme disease was far worse than shivering in the ladies' room at Clingman's Dome.

Not all hikers succumb to the Virginia Blues, though. Bloody Nose, who saw his first bear while making his way up the long Virginia spine, sensed that the Trail Days break had slowed him up some. "Eight of us got back on the Trail on Monday after Trail Days at Virginia 42, Sinking Creek. That afternoon felt like the first day climbing Springer. We had lunch at the Pizza Hut in Pearisburg, then hit the 90 degree heat climbing Sinking Creek Mountain. I almost got ill. But the last few days I have gotten back into the rhythm and am really loving Trail life. I'm taking more and more pictures as the flowers bloom and the snakes and the lizards come out to sun themselves. Virginia Blues is a bunch of hooey." Zamboni Tow-Step concurred. "You couldn't prove the Virginia Blues by me. I'm going to make this hike last as long as I can. There's too much to enjoy. Like the other night. We started hiking at 2:30 in the morning, from Brown Mountain Creek shelter to Cold Mountain for the sunrise. It was magnificent. Just as the sun began to rise, the moon began to set. We got to see both. Now how often do you ever get to see that?"

Trail Gimp enjoyed her night hike to Iron Mountain shelter also, though she was still walking on a bum ankle. "Lil Engine, Yogi, Squirrel, Snowman, Brandon, and I decided to try a night hike. We hit the Trail at 11 P.M. The stars were out and it was a beautiful night. . . . About a mile before reaching the shelter, we all arrived at a clearing and all automatically stopped. It was absolutely beautiful. We saw the whole sky, looked at the stars, and off in the valley we saw the lights of what we figured was the town of Shady Valley, Virginia. As I pulled into the shelter at 3 A.M., I thought about what I would be doing at home on a Saturday night, probably out partying still. I couldn't help but think I was having a better time out here. Figure that."

Annapurna had a similar insightful moment in Chestnut Knob Shelter. "It has been raining off and on since 6 A.M. and this shelter is so cozy I'm in no hurry to leave. The past few days I've been reworking my mail drop schedule to minimize the number of days of food I'm carrying, and once again I am in awe of how long and exciting this Trail is. It fills my heart with joy to think of all that awaits."

Sometimes the kindness of a local resident breaks the grip of mental fatigue. For Cajun C and Screamin Knees, the blues were broken when a local person came by, gave them some cold beer and chips. They decided to take a break, rest up, and swim a little. Soon they had their hiking legs back.

Meanwhile, the northern edge of thru-hikers had something else besides Virginia Blues to contend with. They had Ward Leonard.

"Running into him on the Trail is always a possibility because he spends nearly all of his time there," said Sir Goober Peas. "Supposedly Ward is schizophrenic. Other than this, most people have wildly different stories to tell of him, because he never seems to have the same interaction with more than one person.

"Early in our hike, we heard Ward was 'on the Trail.' In fact we were told that he was responsible for the missing shelter registers throughout the South. Apparently he didn't appreciate what people were writing about him.

"A week ahead of us, he was arrested for wreaking havoc at the Blackburn Center in Northern Virginia. We finally started catching up to him in central Pennsylvania, and were only one day behind at Duncannon. Blue Iggy and Stray Dog had spent some time with him in the Duncannon Laundromat, so we were well aware that our Ward encounter was imminent. The next day we just missed him, but our friends Blue Iggy, Sweet Pea and Stray Dog had hiked nearly all day with him, only to have Ward blow up at Dick Tobias, proprietor of the Bleu Blaze Hostel and storm off in a huff before AJ and I arrived.

"The next day, in some of the hottest weather we experienced on the hike, we were relaxing at the 501 shelter, reading shelter literature and waiting for the caretaker to arrive home so we could gobble down some ice cream sandwiches. Ward strode up to the shelter, and having already met the rest of our group, which now included Bedouin, he didn't introduce himself. But his appearance and mannerism left little doubt who this stranger was. Despite the 90 degree heat, he was wearing long polypro black leggings, a dark blue shirt with long sleeves, and a two-flap safari hat that covered the back of his neck. He carried a small black backpack and held his shirt cuffs in his balled up fists; he walked up to us nearly hunched over, excess sunscreen giving his face and red complexion a pale ghostly look.

"Immediately he started talking, primarily to Sweet Pea, but generally to anyone who would lend an ear. On and on he went, from last night's blow up and the Bleu Blaze Hostel to his philosophy on the AT. I was listening, and unlike the others, had yet to have my fill of Ward's rambling. I started asking him some questions and enjoyed listening to his explanations of why he thru-hikes and why the AT is so much better than the PCT [Pacific Coast Trail].

"Ward is from a distinguished family and he proudly points out that his great, great grandfather was a U.S. Senator. When he learned that we were 'the Cornell Crew' he struck a litany of praise for Ivy League institutions. I could not believe what I was hearing; even some of my friends who are so high on this group of schools could not hold us in higher esteem. Many of his relatives went to Harvard and Brown and Ward made a point to meet as many Ivy League hikers as possible. In fact, he went on to recite a whole list of people from Ivy League schools he had met on the Trail. No doubt we would soon be added to it.

"I had heard Ward was not going to thru-hike this year and asked him why. A major reason was that he felt there was too much pressure to be the first to hike the Trail 11 times. He and Warren Doyle hiked their 10th hike in 1995 and Ward felt that he'd wait until Doyle did his 11th, so he could also complete another thru-hike. I unfortunately forgot to point out that if he were the first to reach 10, why couldn't he break new frontiers again? Another and much weirder reason was that he had seen a large black bear in northern Pennsylvania. Ward doesn't bring a stove, and often has canned food late at night, so he sometimes spills its all over himself. He felt that the combination of tuna oil and black bears was a bad sign, and that this was not to be the year of another thru-hike.

"As AJ and I sat down to dinner, Ward kept talking, in fact sitting right across from us. We both wanted a peaceful meal and didn't know how to go about getting him to leave or at least shut up. Finally AJ said, 'Do you mind leaving us alone, we have some things to discuss.' Without a peep, he stood up, flung on his pack, and said, 'You guys are from Cornell, so I wouldn't want to mess with you.'

"And just like that, he was off like a spook in the night."

j u n e

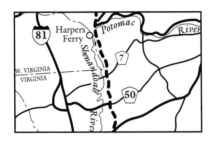

IF YOU DON'T GET UP AND WALK,
THEN YOU WON'T GET TO KATAHDIN.

-The Cat in the Hat

T he ranks of thru-hikers were indeed becoming smaller, but by the time June rolled in, the thru-hikers still on the Trail were poised to come full and happy stride into Harper's Ferry, West Virginia, home of the headquarters of the Appalachian Trail Conference. Up ahead the leading edge of hikers was pushing through Pennsylvania.

June, of course, is the month when the hiking should be easy. The snows have stopped, the birds sing, the trees provide relief from the sun. The days are pleasantly warm at higher elevations and the nights can be wonderfully cool. Long summer days mean that hikers can enjoy hiking early in the morning and late into the evening and treat themselves to lazy, mid-day breaks, preferably near a creek or swimming hole, without worrying too much about whether they're making the miles. Besides, as Pony Express pointed out, "If you crawled over all of those hills in Georgia and North Carolina, you know you can get through Virginia." Hikers have found their rhythm.

For many hikers, Harper's Ferry is the psychological halfway point, and indeed the landscape, with the magnificent confluence of the Potomac and Shenandoah Rivers, sends out a powerful signal that a symbolic line is about to be crossed. The building in Harper's Ferry that houses the Appalachian Trail Conference, however, is as unassuming and unpretentious as the volunteer effort that protects, maintains, and otherwise shepherds the Trail. Two levels high and built of stone, the office is a constant stage for hikers to come in, introduce themselves, get their pictures made and, in keeping with the spirit of the Appalachian Trail, donate some of their day to help do whatever needs to be done. It is the heart of an independent community of hikers. As one of Zamboni Tow-Step's stats indicated:

"Four—the number of people you have to smile at to get someone to smile back in Anytown, USA.

"One—the number of people you have to smile in Harper's Ferry to get someone to smile at you."

As hikers come in off the Trail, remove their packs and go inside, packs decorate the front porch. It's a scene oddly reminiscent of months earlier in Georgia where packs decorated car bumpers. However, now

Rita, Home Brew, Blueberry, and Cat in the Hat at the ATC entrance. Harper's Ferry, West Virginia.

there is a difference. Once clean packs sport a fine layer of truly ground-in dirt and they sag in all of the right places. The external packs that some hikers carry are thoroughly scratched and eyelets and rivets look loose. Even when the packs are not riding proudly on the backs of thru-hikers, they perfume the air with *eau de Trail bacpaquer*, a smell very much like damp life-preservers.

The hikers are also different. Gone is the nervous, mill-about energy that causes them to kick cement curbing with their boots. In Harper's Ferry, thru-hikers can be still as they wait for a ride to appear. Gone are the furtive looks of hikers sizing up each other and their respective gear. In Harper's Ferry, hikers wear confident, broad smiles. They're loving living outside. Who cares if noses red from the cold have given way to legs covered with bug bites? Who cares that their boots are beginning to resemble something dragged over dirt roads and fought over by feral dogs? These people have earned their confidence and pride; to call them merely 'field-tested' is an understatement. They are hill- and rock- and wind- and cold- and wet- and hunger- and blister- and pain-tested. "You always hurt," stated Will-Make-It. The Cat in the Hat agreed, "Some part of your body always hurts." Allgood coped with the dull ache of his collar bone everyday when he hoisted up his pack to go. Hikers rise above the pain, telling themselves that "pain is Nature's way of letting weakness escape the body."

In many cases the hikers who have made it this far are those who have learned to listen to their bodies. "Hiking is 90 percent head, 10 percent heel," observed Julie McCoy, Cruise Director. Looking down at her knee brace, she cautioned, "You gotta listen to your body. I have a sore knee after putting in a 20 mile day I shouldn't have put in. And I don't always stay on the Trail. If I want a Pepsi, I get off the Trail, hike into town, and get a Pepsi." In other cases, they are the hikers who have consistently trimmed pack weight. "I started with 80 pounds," laughed Allgood. "Eighty pounds! Can you believe it? But now I'm down to 50." And what did he get rid of? "All sorts of stuff. I didn't get anybody to help me, though, because I knew I needed to figure it out for myself." And some hikers looked for the comedy in their aches and pains, finding it amusing that duct tape, the all purpose blister fixer, had a dual purpose. "It leaves gummy stuff on your toes, and then fuzzy stuff like sock lint and sleeping bag grunge sticks to the gummy stuff. Man, I can get the dust outta my sleeping bag just by using my feet," chuckled Walk with Wong.

Unlike the register in Amicalola, Georgia, with its tentative, hopeful, and brief comments, the Trail register in the Appalachian Trail Office fairly shouts with a verbal celebration of accomplishment, as hiker after hiker who has walked this far takes a moment to write his or her thoughts upon arriving in Harper's Ferry. Some are quite amazed that they've made it this far: "Apostle John is proud of himself" reads one entry and "Now I feel like we can call ourselves thru-hikers. Hard to believe that we've done close to 1000 miles. Then again, our feet can believe it," wrote the Canadian Geese. Kilroy took it all in, writing, "I'm sitting here in utter amazement. Yes, I'm in Harper's Ferry. I bet I look like I never hiked anywhere when I get back on the Trail—new boots, no poison ivy, no bug bites, no beard, nothing that says 'hiker trash.' Yes that means I won't stink either."

For some thru-hikers, the wonder of the achievement moves them to poetry, something they may never have known was inside, as Seldom Seen showed. "Have you ever just walked through the woods, or sat on a rock and watched the clear blue sky through a thick green forest canopy? Have you ever slept under the stars or walked through a cloud or listened to raindrops trickle off of the leaves and onto the ground, or have you ever heard the whippoorwill tell its lonesome story at night or listened to what the trees and the animals have to say, or just heard the leaves rustle in the wind? I have for the past few couple of months and it's a good feeling, knowing that if I got off the Trail tomorrow, I would have lived today."

As early season hikers strode into and beyond Harper's Ferry, as mid-season hikers either enjoyed Virginia or battled the blues, and late season hikers closed in on Damascus, something went terribly wrong and June 1996 became a month vastly different than it should have been.

To be sure, the first few days and nights of June were wonderful and the hikers who were in Shenandoah National Park were enjoying its relatively flat stretches, the occasional smell of honeysuckle, the butterflies, the waist high ferns, and the thickening green tunnel through which they walked. Hikers walked beside and under blooming mountain laurel and watched for wild turkeys and wobbly newborn fawns. Trail friendships continued to deepen into a strong sense of family as hikers shared their wilderness world with each other.

For Blue Sky and company, the night of June 3 was especially memorable. A group of '96 hikers had met a '92 hiker the night before at the Tom Floyd shelter and together planned a cookout. "We planned it for the Jim and Molly Denton shelter, one of the best on the Trail. We all packed items to grill in from Front Royal, only five miles from the shelter. The spread of food and drinks we had there was truly amazing. We had beer, chicken, steak, chips, cookies, burgers, hot dogs, and everything you could want for a party. We even had music supplied by a portable disc played and small speakers. It was by far the best night of fellowship I've had on the Trail. We even had ice cream floats [Tarkus, a '92 thru-hiker, had hiked in two 10 pound bags of charcoal and later showed up with ice cream and sodas to make the floats]. This night [could] not be beat. It was the right combination of friendship, food and love for the outdoors." Big Dipper, Navigator, Gumby, Turdle, Bird, Firefly, The Apostles, and Entropy would surely agree with him.

However, this Eden was shattered when word went out that two hikers had been murdered in Shenandoah National Park.

On June 4, the *Washington Post* reported that two women were "found slain in Shenandoah National Park." The women were found by rangers Saturday night within three miles of Skyland Lodge. The women had had their throats slashed; to the Park authorities it was clearly a homicide even thought they struggled to pinpoint when the crime took place. Reports fixed it as early as May 23 or perhaps as late as May 31. Although officials believed it to be an isolated incident, they had precious few clues and as late as a week later were still groping for significant leads.

The slain women were not thru-hikers, but their bodies were found close enough to the Appalachian Trail to rattle hikers who were in the park during the time the women were murdered. Even if the murders had occurred elsewhere on another trail in another park, the reaction would have been much the same. The family of Appalachian Trail hikers feels its bonds deeply and when Nature's sanctuary is violated in a manner such as this, there is a collective ache for the loss.

Gumby and Turdle, who just the night before had celebrated a wonderful wilderness cookout, realized just how close to the scene of the crime they were. Gumby said in a hushed voice that it was entirely possible that he might have stepped outside a campsite only to trip over the women's bodies. That next night, the hikers held a moment of silence to the memory of the dead women. It mattered not in the least that no current thru-hikers knew them. The women were lovers of the outside, of the natural world that the thru-hikers feel akin to, and that was enough.

But a moment of silence could hardly lay the matter to rest. Hikers who were nearing Shenandoah were by turns angry and scared. Many packed in at Rusty's Hard Time Hollow to await more news. Midnight was angry because "someone has taken not only two lives but also our freedom to enjoy the Trail the way we want to. No longer can we stop and camp at a beautiful spot or because we're tired and want to stop for the day. Instead we must push on to the shelters where there is safety in numbers. We came out here to experience the Trail, the people and all of God's beauty, but I feel now that we're just putting in miles and looking over our shoulders. What a shame that so many lives have been touched by one senseless and cruel crime. We will continue with our hike however, and try each day to put this out of our mind and see all that is around us and remember that each step is fulfilling our dream."

Reactions to the murder were all over the board. Mr. Bean observed the effect of the news on the thru-hiking women and while recognizing that you "always have to be aware of strangers," he hoped that "they don't get off the Trail because of it." Spare, a hiker who reached Shenandoah just a few days after the reports went out, solved the safety issue by walking along the Skyline Drive, saying that "the AT nearly parallels the Skyline Drive, so since I'm by myself and I don't want to stop, this seemed like the best compromise. I just felt uneasy on the Trail, always looking over my shoulder. It's hard to hike that way."

Further down the Virginia spine, near Bland, Rogue Bear remarked that "reports of two women murdered in Shenandoah has thru-hikers around here worried. We're two weeks away from there and with the 'escaped convict' situation on our minds, it makes us wonder what's happening." As far south as Pearisburg, hikers were shaken. Reported BB and the Purple Pirate, "We're still on the Trail, although the last stretch was a little weird after hearing about the murders in the Shenandoahs. Two hikers we know left the Trail at Bland because of it. Us, we're just looking for someone large and menacing-looking to hike with through the Park. We're not that scared, but definitely a little shaken up." Sweet Dreams was shaken also: "This is frightening! Poor them. Poor family. We are all upset, and I hope they catch this crazy murderer pretty soon."

Certainly authorities were investigating. A $25,000 reward was offered and agents had been brought in from as far away as Yellowstone National Park. Trail registers were confiscated from the huts to be read for clues, and many of the thru-hikers who had been in the Park reported that their families had been contacted and questioned by the FBI. Some hikers saw armed rangers patrolling the Trail. Spare was convinced that a female agent, duded up as a thru-hiker, was out on the Trail trying to wheedle information out of thru-hikers. "She looked at me and said that she wasn't afraid, that she had a big knife with her. I guess she thought that if I were the killer I was going to compare knives with her."

One hiker, Mr. Bean, felt the full force of the investigation when he arrived at Panorama, a restaurant at Thornton Gap popular with tourists and hikers alike. As he sat taking a break and studying a map, Mr. Bean was approached by an agent.

"Mr. Bean?"

"Yes."

"Dick Doucette?"

"Yes."

Immediately on guard that the agent could know this much about him from his appearance—and wondering if he resembled the killer—Mr. Bean proceeded to answer questions that the agent asked. Questions seemed intent on testing Mr. Bean's knowledge of the Trail, as if to get a read on just long he'd been on it.

"Where is this Appalachian Trail?"

"Just over there," answered Mr. Bean.

"Is it that wide everywhere?"

"No. Sometimes it's narrow and sometimes it's wide enough for two people. But mostly it's meant for one at a time."

"Is it always that flat?"

"No, sometimes it goes uphill and then it goes downhill."

"Is it always that level?"

"No, sometimes it's full of rocks and sometimes it's root bound."

"How long have you been on the Trail, Mr. Bean?"

"I started March 24."

And so it went for 30 minutes. The agent finally admitted he'd been watching Mr. Bean for two days, and thanked him for his time. He concluded by saying that he *wouldn't* be in touch again. Mr. Bean was left to wonder if he bore any resemblance to the suspected killer.

Not all thru-hikers were scared, but nearly all were angry about the murder, for reasons that others might find difficult to understand. Long distance hiking requires that the hiker become both adept and comfortable with making independent decisions about how to handle certain situations. Long distance hikers are not the kind of people who look to others to tell them how to cope with the things Life throws at them. Hikers in Virginia in 1995, for example, had had to figure out how to navigate many rivers that were flooding up out of their banks. Either they made careful and calculated decisions, or they risked possible injury and perhaps even death. Making decisions of this sort is simply a part of the long-distance hiking experience that hikers welcome and accept. The way they see it, there is little opportunity for personal challenge if hard decisions are removed from the experience. Earlier in 1996, hikers had been forced to consider their chances of survival while camping in zero temperatures with wind chills lower than that. Now, confronted with a murder and the distinct possibility that the murderer (or murderers) was still in the vicinity, thru-hikers were angry that officials seemed to be withholding what little information there was to be had. Not shirking from making these difficult decisions, the thru-hikers wanted to know as much as possible so that they could decide for themselves what to do and then accept the consequences.

Firefly said it best. "I was in the area when it happened. I was actually with the rangers when they began to get clues as to where the missing girls were. . . . Many people have criticized me for continuing my hike and my parents for allowing me to make this decision. But I want you all to consider for a minute what it is like driving on the Beltway. People are killed there *daily*, yet we all continue to get in our cars. The Appalachian Trail has had nine murders in the 50 years of its existence. Millions of people hike on this trail each season. Now, yes, there is still danger. There is danger in walking down your neighborhood street. But you take the precautions and do it.

"I am a smart girl. I know some are worried because I am alone. But you must understand, I am never really alone. The Trail is like a giant family. People are watching me from all directions at all times. I am always well accounted for."

Another problem was that good information got lost inside misinformation, and hikers didn't know whom to believe. "A woman in Atkins told us that the girls had been in her store," observed Bonnie and Clyde. Even as late as August, *Outside* magazine would report that the murder was of two women who were thru-hiking the Appalachian Trail.

It was regrettable that for the Class of '96 the murders in Shenandoah momentarily overshadowed the beauty of the park in particular and of the hike in general. Walking quickly as a bunch on the Trail, perhaps looking over their shoulders, many hikers were unable to slow down to appreciate the waist high ferns or the purple Virginia spiderwort blooming at their feet. Those hikers who met armed rangers patrolling the Trail in Shenandoah National Park were doubly shocked. What were armed agents doing out there? However, the hikers tried as best they could to put the murders behind them and to focus on other experiences the Trail offers.

Unfortunately for some hikers, what the Trail had to offer was a continuing grind of pain, discomfort, and grime. Trail Gimp noted that she'd "never been this dirty in my life. I can see all of the lines in my hand simply because they are filled with dirt. I wash my hands, but they're still brown." Still trying to walk on her bum ankle, Trail Gimp struggled to get water. "I followed a path down to some rhododendrons to a stream. But what stream? I followed the stream until I came across enough water to filter. I filtered from what I would call at home a 'mud puddle.' But I had to do it." Eventually the grind wore her down. "So I got started thinking: Did I really want to hike the AT, or was I using it as an excuse to get away from my pathetic life at home? I knew some serious soul searching had to happen . . . and if I'm not going to make it to Maine, why prolong the pain?"

For some hikers the Trail offered more time to grapple with the Blues. The way M&M described it, the Blues were almost inevitable. "People are spread out, some hikers have watched their partners quit, and there have been a lot of injuries. As you come into your own pace, you sometimes go for days without seeing people." M&M finally worked through her blues and started enjoying the Trail again. "Now it's so great to see the end of Virginia in sight and the weather has finally been perfect for hiking—sunny and cool. I actually enjoyed getting thoroughly doused by Mother Nature these last 24 hours, since it was a warm rain. It's also been a lot more fun with a partner. I haven't laughed so much in weeks. I'm still searching for a pain-free day of hiking, but I'm having a great time." Wildhair wrestled with his Blues for about two weeks, beating them somewhere, finally, in Pennsylvania. Robohiker fought his since leaving Damascus. "I was totally unmotivated to hike, and didn't leave camp until 3:30 on two consecutive days. But I got over it, due to the AYCE Pizza Hut buffet. A five mile day and 1.5 days off in Troutville seemed to cure my tiredness." Bonnie and Clyde wrestled with their fatigue, wondering "how are we ever going to finish? We thought we knew it all. We read and we read and we read. We lived for five months once in a tent in Alaska." Still the rigors of the AT beat on them until one day, in Waynesboro, they realized that they could finish their hike. "We realized we'd done 26 miles in one day from The Priest."

Some hikers were depressed because the Trail hadn't become easy. Cajun C assessed it realistically. "This Trail doesn't get easy. Sure it rolls, but it's not easy. You still go up and you still go down. And you're still carrying a pack." Nomad concurred, "Everyone said that northern Virginia is flat and easier . . . have yet to see it, and I have only two days left!" BB and the Purple Pirate went head on with their blues, saying "The Virginia Blues have got us down a bit. Only one-third down and a zillion miles to go! But the Trail is home, so we'll keep walking."

Some hikers, such as Walk with Wong, pooh-poohed the notion of the Virginia Blues. "They're just really hot and tired for the first time, and they've been told they're going to be depressed in Virginia. So that's what they think it is." Ranger Dave just chuckled and said, "The Virginia Blues are what happens when you blue-blaze."

Part of coping with the Blues includes coping with pack weight. Though the hikers are admittedly stronger, carrying the pack every day can be a drag. With winter in the past, hikers were able to comfort their backs by shipping home their winter gear. Heavy sleeping bags went home, as did heavy tents. Heavy winter clothing went home. Some hikers, no longer needing the warmth of a hot meal to stave off hypothermia, sent their stoves home. "Tortillas and cereals are my staples now," remarked Nomad. "We'll see how soon I get sick of them." Hikers also begin to refuse pennies as change, or when they do get them, they leave them behind in the shelters. One thru-hiker, refusing her pennies at the Mt. Rogers Visitor Center, simply said, "Pack weight, y'know." Like other hikers, Sir Goober Peas took a different tack. "When thinking of what I wanted and needed to carry, I wondered whether it was worth the worry always to be thinking 'am I traveling as light as possible; if not then what else could I pitch?' Personally I wanted to avoid these anal and distracting thoughts so I could enjoy the hike."

Other hikers had to cope with plain, old, everyday sickness. Nomad fell ill with some crud just out of Harper's Ferry. So did Allgood. "Man, all I could think was 'I'm gonna die here.'" Sweet Dreams noted that "many, many hikers have been sick for the last few days. It's contagious. They throw up, they are not able to eat, they are not able to hike. Some got the giardia, others the flu." Walk with Wong, a doctor, speculated that when hikers fell ill with chills, aches, fever, nausea and other intestinal ailments, it was due to the lack of sanitary conditions. "They're not practicing safe gorp. Man, you can be sitting in a shelter playing cards and someone breaks open the gorp bag and starts passing it around. Probably nobody's washed in days and who knows what's on your hands. You don't want to be unfriendly and not take a handful. But then a week or so later, you turn up sick and wonder why."

A few hikers struggled with the high numbers of people on the Trail. Though many hikers had quit, many were still on the Trail. Highlander decided to skip the central third of the Trail and restart his hike in Connecticut. "I am tired of all the people on the Trail. They are interesting, but it's too crowded and the Trail through Virginia to New York is too close to roads and towns. I'm giving up my thru-hike to enjoy myself more, and just plan on going from Connecticut to Maine. Not having to worry about schedules and making miles will allow me to enjoy my hike more."

Another problem that sneaked up on a few hikers was the pull of home and relationships. Many non-hikers harbor the notion that long-distance hikers are somehow hermits and recluses. Nothing could be further from the truth. While they are quite independent, hikers are quite capable of cherishing hearth and home. Damn Near Bootless, one fine June morning just out of Harper's Ferry, found that homestrings had seized the upper hand. With a single tear rolling slowly down her cheek, Bootless said that, "Leaving someone for six months is something not to be taken lightly. I miss my husband. We've been married for 27 years and he's a wonderful companion. It isn't that I'm not having fun. I'm having a wonderful time. I've met so many wonderful people out here. You might think you come out here for the independence and freedom, but when someone in a shelter passes you a cup of hot tea and that tea helps you resist hypothermia, or someone lights your stove for you because you're too cold and you can't, you realize how dependent upon people you are. And you develop a bond that's incredible. But I also have a bond with my husband and that's important too. So now I think I might flip-flop. That way I can go to Maine and start hiking toward Harper's Ferry and complete my hike that way and he can come with me. If I'm clever, I think I can make this work and have both: company with my husband and the wonders of the Trail."

Zenwalker was likewise wrestling with the pull of loved ones. In Harper's Ferry, waiting for his girlfriend to arrive, Zenwalker looked off into the distance and said, when asked if he'd had enough, "Well, I've had a lot, that's for sure. I just didn't realize I was going to miss her as much as I do." Within a month, Trail rumor had it that Zenwalker had left the Trail and proposed marriage.

Trail life wasn't without comedy as hikers coped with how different thru-hiking was making them. Cajun C and Screamin Knees left the Trail for a few days to attend a friend's wedding. "It looked like we lost all of our social skills. We just sat back in a corner and talked to each other. We didn't really know what to say to other people." Zamboni and Speedo had a similar, albeit different, experience. One day at a shelter they met two very comely, novice hikers—the new gear and boots gave the women away. One was clearly having trouble with her stove. It was new and she didn't quite know how to use it. So Zamboni and Speedo offered to show her. Because they'd been on the Trail for so long, they weren't really sure how to keep the conversation going. One of the women broke the awkwardness, asking "so what's it like to be a thru-hiker?"

"Oh, we put in long days, lots of miles," replied Zamboni.

"Really?"

"Yeah, we put in 20 miles on an average day."

"Really? Why?"

"Well, if you want to get to Katahdin, you have to put in some big days."

Deciding to put his two cents' worth in, Speedo chirped up, adding, "And we don't even use toilet paper anymore."

The conversation stopped and the girls reportedly moved to the far side of the shelter. Zamboni and Speedo left early the next morning so that their paths wouldn't cross again. It was probably good that the lack of underwear wasn't mentioned. Neither party was interested in revisiting the underwear question.

Although many hikers found it necessary to stop and wrestle with their own personal demons and challenges, many were able to work through them and keep walking northward and to experience other 'joys of the Trail.' 'Joys of the Trail' is both simple and difficult to explain, but it is a real and powerful part of the thru-hiker experience, and throughout June, from the Delaware Water Gap to somewhere in Virginia, thru-hikers were absorbing these pleasures.

On one level it describes the fun that hikers have together, like the evening when Bag Lady camped out on the steps of the Mount Rogers Visitors' Center with 25 other hikers. "We slept on the porch, ordered pizza from the Sugar Grove Diner. It was fun to stay with so many people and have good non-trail food." It describes eating a "real" lunch at Big Meadows Lodge and then sitting outside to enjoy an afternoon break. It's sitting on a bench at a gas station and gasping as the cold fizz of a really cold can of soda tickles the roof of your mouth and back of your throat. It's waking up to the serenade of birds' songs at 5 A.M., when all of them sing the song each know best and the symphony of it all resembles the ongoing clatter of silverware hitting the floor and all of it is wonderful. It's walking with Bounce tucked into your pack and hat to keep away the bugs and realizing that you'd never, ever go to the mall this way. It's night hiking under a full moon. ("There's a little more adrenaline in your system that pushes you faster. It must be some primal fear thing. All I know was that the view from the Dragon's Tooth on a full moon was awesome!" exclaimed Walk with Wong.) And it's certainly the immediate, cool

Halfway point of the Appalachian Trail.
Pine Grove Furnace State Park, Pennsylvania.

feeling feet have when they are liberated from the socks and sock liners they have been wearing. Unequaled!

Certainly the joys of the Trail include stops at places like Woodshole and Rusty's. "This place was magic, wonderful, fantastic," recalled Sweet Dreams about her stay at Woodshole. "When you enter this land you feel so in peace with yourself. Tillie makes our journey easier."

For early season hikers, it includes the sense of accomplishment and celebration they have when they cross not only the psychological halfway point but also the physical halfway point, just south of Pine Grove Furnace State Park, in Pennsylvania. There the verbal celebration in the Trail registers continues as hikers leave entries behind to perk up the hikers who will follow. Poly + Ester left this rhyme of celebration:

Yahoo, wahoo, flounder and trout!
Now here is the sign to cheer the down and out!
Not that the two of us are hitting any lows—
We're as high as two kites and the wacky joy shows!

Brush likewise left a poem of his own:

The halfway point
Has found me quite grand.
I hope those who follow
Can understand

The wonder and joy
I've found upon this day
Can only truly be appreciated
By those who walk this way.

Other hikers understate their pride. Nomad, amazed at his progress, especially given his earlier sickness in Harper's Ferry, simply noted, "Damn, this is a long way." Bones and Little Tree felt the same: "Never thought we'd see the day." Big Dipper was looking forward to the next 1,069 miles, writing, "One day shy of three months to this point. I always play better on the back nine!" And of course, hiker humor, never in short supply, isn't lacking in Harper's Ferry. One hiker simply asked, "Halfway where? Can I change my socks now?"

As hikers stride past the halfway point, many of them try their stomachs at a challenge issued by the camp store in Pine Grove Furnace State Park: eat a half-gallon of ice cream in one sitting upon coming into the park and win a wooden spoon. Although many hikers chose chocolate, Nomad ate peach, and Wildhair tried his hand at wild cherry. Not every hiker was successful at downing the half-gallon of ice cream.

"Trail joys" can also describe the anticipation thru-hikers have when they approach a well-known and much celebrated thru-hiker hangout, like the Doyle Hotel in Duncannon, Pennsylvania. "Da Doyle," as thru-hikers affectionately call it, is a crumbling Victorian, now-condemned hotel, complete with peeling paint on the outside and "Unsafe" signs taped on the columns that support the second floor balcony. It's where, as Marmot put it, "thru-hikers check out, but they can never leave" and the regulars show up at the horseshoe-shaped bar about 8:30 each morning. But it doesn't matter, really, for the people are friendly and the beer is cheap. "'Da Doyle awaits—beer, sausages and brats. Life is good and only getting gooder," noted Apostle Luke, as he looked forward to the hike into Duncannon.

It's the satisfaction felt when a hiker indulges his childlike curiosity and looks inside the hiker box, a beat up cardboard box that seems to be a fixture in nearly every shelter. You just never know what you're going to discover in the hiker box: pretzels, crossword puzzle books, tweezers, maps, Werther's butterscotch. There could be anything.

It includes the offbeat hiker humor: like Singe, who was collecting toenails other hikers lost (this often happens when hikers develop blisters underneath their toenails) and stringing them on dental floss for a necklace. "Yeah, he wants to get a set of 10 so he can tell everybody they're his," laughed Walk with Wong and Pony Express.

It's what made Zamboni Tow-Step say, after pouring a half of a cup of water out of his boots and wringing nearly as much out of his socks, "I'm staying out here as long as possible. I want to make this experience last."

On quite another level, however, the joys of the Trail refer to the Trail Magic that the hikers continue to encounter, like the generosity that Allgood and Marmot experienced at the Thursday night feast hosted by the Church of the Mountain in Delaware Water Gap. "It was so nice to see the community support for thru-hikers. One hiker went to the end of the line for seconds and everyone made him go to the front of the line. 'Hikers first!' they all said." Lives there a thru-hiker who doesn't melt at an invitation such as this? Or like Ajax, who fell sick and was taken to doctors in Front Royal, Virginia, by Trail maintainers in the Potomac Appalachian Trail Club. "Trail maintainers, other hikers, everyone has been top notch." Or like Lea and Steve who, upon crossing Pickle Branch in mid-Virginia, met Dewey Houck. "He was out checking on his cabin and about to head home. He let us in, turned on the water pump for us, told us we could stay for the night and to pull the lock tight in the morning." Occasionally it's the doughnuts left in plastic bags on trees or apples stashed in a bag or beer tucked discreetly in a cold stream, all left anonymously, of course. "We can always go see the mountains," the Hiking Vikings said, "it's the people who make this Trail special."

Sometimes it's the Trail Magic that happens at special places. All of the hikers appreciated the Williams' goodie tree near Hogpen Gap, Virginia. "When I think of the money Ed and Mary Williams are spending just to put gas in his van to drive up and down those hills just to leave the treats, I'm amazed," said Ranger Dave. Sprout and nine other hikers also experienced a little Magic at the half point marker. "Rumor had it that a school teacher who had been on the Trail a couple of days earlier heard about the crazy Trail Magic stories and wanted to get in on the fun. We'd heard that he'd decided that he was going to bring pizza, beer and sodas. We all arrived about 7 P.M., around the time he said he'd be there. By 7:10, there hadn't been a sign. We made conversation, but all of our attention was focused on the side trail leading to the shelter. A squirrel would rustle the leaves and everybody's heads would whip around in anticipation only to be shot down when we realized what it was. Seven fifteen, seven-twenty five, tick-tock, tick-tock. Seven thirty came and we all took out our Whisperlites. It looked like we were going to have to eat mac and cheese again. At 7:40 someone said, 'I think it's them.' It couldn't be. But it was though. This man had driven an hour in a rainstorm and walked a mile up a hill with pizzas and a huge cooler of beer, soda, and ice. Yahoo! Trail Magic lives! We all literally jumped and boogied in glee. What an amazing way to celebrate the midway point—with friends, and Trail Angels. Kindness, generosity seem to be abundant—no—*are* abundant on this Trail!"

Sometimes hikers happen upon a local celebration and are able to join in the fun. At the last minute, Craigmont ponied up a buck to enter the drawing for a $25.00 prize during the fund-raiser held at the Union House in Port Clinton for the Vietnam War memorial. Moments later, he was announced the winner. At Gathland State park in Maryland, Screamin Knees and Cajun C happened upon the 100th anniversary of the War Correspondents' Arch and were invited to partake of the food and ice cream.

For some it's the impromptu parties that the Trail community pitches. Recalled Sneakers, "Nantahala to Fontana Dam had been the worst section yet. We've dubbed it 'Nantahella.' The climb up to Cheoah Bald was straight up 3,500 feet in less than 8 miles. From here, the trail followed the ridge and is straight up, straight down, no switchbacks. But we had some Trail Magic waiting at the Fontana Hilton. Lethal Pastor, who hiked with us to Nantahala, was waiting with everything the hiker wants—beer, chips, cookies, cheese, doughnuts, fruit, you name it. What an evening."

Occasionally Trail Magic is simply the timely and much-needed help that arrives on the unseen wings of a kind person. Marv of the Hiking Vikings experienced it on the front porch of the Appalachian Trail

Conference office in Harper's Ferry. Having some tremendous foot pain, Marv needed to see a podiatrist. Allison Alsdorf, a local Trail Angel, happened to overhear his plight and offered him her car keys. With a phone book in his lap, he called out to her, "You're a wonderful Trail Angel!" Shrugging her shoulders she smiled and then shouted back, "I've just learned that what you give has a way of coming back!" Many hikers experienced Trail Magic when they hiked upon the reconstructed Chesapeake and Ohio Towpath. The towpath had been severely damaged by the January floods earlier in the year, so much so that as late as April that portion of the Trail looked to be closed. However, due to efforts by the volunteer Trail crews, a generous donation by Amoco, and the loan of front-end loaders from the National Park Service, the towpath was passable.

For people who just three months earlier stepped out of a world that often seems focused on legislating anonymous programs to do good deeds instead of letting people extend the personal kindnesses they see fit, Trail Magic reawakens the thru-hikers' own spirit of spontaneous generosity. Some hikers are so profoundly affected by the Trail Magic they experience that they promise to return the favor somewhere along the way. Cygnus Swan, writing to Bob and Ruth in Port Clinton, Pennsylvania, said, "You've touched a sweet part of my spirit with your warm talk and actions, as well as your cold ice cream. I will spread this magic into the 'other world.' You can count on me."

Certainly hikers prize these grand, spontaneous acts of generosity that flow from the plain, everyday people of the Trail community, but they are not the only ingredient in Trail joys. Strong among the Trail joys is a growing and closer connection with nature, however and wherever a hiker chooses to see it. For Annapurna, it was a bit of modern whimsy held in a rustic setting: "This place—Holy Family Hostel—is so beautiful. There's an old wooden barn with a kitchen, bathroom, and library/study with a sleeping loft and a large, expansive lawn for camping. This morning those of us at the hostel made a pot of coffee and danced to oldies on the little radio. I received a letter from a friend, and read this quote from Walt Whitman: 'Now I see the secret of the making of the best persons. It is to grow in the open air and to eat and sleep with the earth.'"

Bandana Light experienced moments of this same feeling and attempted to explain his metaphysical experience: "It sometimes feels as if I'm a character in a Winnie the Pooh story. The way the Trail winds through the pine trees, I could be on my way to Christopher Robin's house." Then pausing to reflect upon this, Bandana Light continued,

"There are so many bright, creative, educated, innovative people who are thru-hikers. It's got to make you wonder what the 'other world' is lacking that they get from being out here. After the physical pain and the joy of pure escapism passes it becomes a journey of the soul. At times I have been walking along and just started to laugh, feeling joy from existing, from connection with the natural world."

Of course, some Trail joys are fairly basic and remind thru-hikers that not everything about the Trail experience is intellectual or spiritual. Like eating, for example. In the 'other world' people live their lives, as Sweet Dreams observed, "looking at the nutrition facts in order to buy low fat and low calorie food." But on the Trail, it's the opposite. "If there's a lot of calories and fat, we buy it and eat it with pleasure." A Quanee marveled at his own ability to eat:

Catfish experiencing some Trail joy in Damascus, Virginia.

"While at The Home-place in Catawba, I had four plates of fried chicken, mashed potatoes, corn, slaw with a few biscuits, two servings of peach cobbler with ice cream. Later I had one orange creamsicle, one fudge pop, one pint of milk, six Oreo cookies, one Rice Krispy treat, half a pack of Mentos and numerous chips. Oh yeah, and before dinner I ate one small bag of chips and a quart of Gatorade." Ranger Dave seconded that opinion, saying "I've been in a lot of restaurants all around the world and for country home cooking it is excellent." Breaking Wind, upon exiting the all-you-can-eat buffet at the

Hilltop House in Harper's Ferry, plopped down into the overstuffed sofa and exhaled a sigh of pure joy. "Four hours of food," he said. "It was wonderful. Absolutely wonderful. We started at lunch and ate through dinner." In Boiling Springs, Accorn described his experience. "I came, I saw, I ate, I'm going into a food comatose; that's done, I go." Will-Make-It, who swore that after several months on the Trail he could both see and taste double cheeseburgers, recalled the day he came into Damascus. "My feet were screaming. I'd put in 26 miles. When I came in, I got a 20 ounce Pepsi and a six pack of Snickers bars. I drank that Pepsi and ate four Snickers bars and got up and bought another Pepsi. It was wonderful." Craigmont summed up the all-you-can-eat experience. "You do it and it's wonderful. Then you feel terrible. Laughing, he added, "But you do it again every chance you get!"

Throughout June the leading edge of hikers pushed their way north, passing through the beautiful farmlands of Pennsylvania. With the passing of days, the summer heat kicked in. Since Nature had failed at freezing the hikers, was She now going to bake them? It appeared so. Temperatures pushed well above 90 and hikers watched blue skies turn milky with humidity. "It's freakin' hot," noted Snowshoes. Finding water became difficult, and hikers paid for it. Sweaty, sticky, smelly, dehydrated, the hikers were lucky to reach the gentler terrain of the mid-Atlantic states.

The traverse of farmland was quite a change from the mountains and ridges they had been following. On a daily basis they saw great wood and stone barns decorated with Pennsylvania Dutch hex signs and spires that evoked images of Germanic castles. Was Misfit in Oz when he passed through the Great Valley of Pennsylvania? "Yesterday I was lulled to sleep by the acres of waving fields of farmland, so I stopped to take a nap. When I woke I thought 'Good God, I'm lost in a field of wheat. It could be weeks before I ever find my way out.' Then I stood up and realized it was only three feet tall. Close shave that time."

Some hikers used the farmland stretch to put in big mileage days. A Wink and A Smile were "quickly passing through. Our first 27 mile day. Ouchie, ouchie." Craigmont, coming through later noted that it was his "10th 27 mile day. Ibuprofen, ibuprofen." Wildhair wanted to see if he could put in a 30 mile day. He did, but developed shin splints and a golf ball-sized knot on his leg. "I vowed never to do another one of those," he noted. Not all of the hikers enjoyed the flat stretches, though. "Turbo was perturbo during yesterday's farmland hike."

After passing through the Pennsylvania farmland, hikers rolled into Duncannon and then crossed the Susquehanna River to start the ridge walking Pennsylvania is known for. Into Port Clinton they hiked, stopping to quaff the locally brewed Yuengling beer either at the Port Clinton Hotel or at the Union House. And that's when they experienced a yet another Pennsylvania, for it is past Port Clinton, that Pennsylvania turns into Rocksylvania. And indeed the rocks are legendary. According to hikers, this part of Pennsylvania is "where boots go to die." Gutsy, upon encountering the rocks, said "I'd been cheated [by the rocks I'd been promised] up until now."

These rocks, sharp and unforgiving, are left over from glaciers that once extended into the area. Like little rain drops spitting just before a downpour breaks, the rocks make their appearance slowly. At first hikers might think that "hey, this isn't so bad." Gradually the rocks become more plentiful until finally what was a dirt and root-bound path resembles a river of dirty little icebergs locked into the earth. Sometimes the rocks run parallel to the path like dorsal fins. Sometimes just the jagged sharp top of an asymmetrical obelisk points upward from the ground. Sometimes the rocks, sitting upright and crossways on the Trail like headstones, are at just the right angle to catch a boot toe. Sometimes they lie flat, and even that's deceptive because they shift back and forth and can pitch a hiker from the Trail.

Even though most hikers wear boots designed to protect their feet, the rocks make their presence undeniably known. Inside a boot, a foot lies generally cradled, ready to pivot up and down at the ankle to take a step. On a Pennsylvania rock, the foot, trying to hold up a hiker and an extra 20–40 pounds, begins to crease and fold in ways a foot was never meant to crease or fold. It is as if the rocks find a way first to crease the foot lengthwise and then to crease it across, until finally, up in the center of the foot, there comes an ache like no other. It isn't a surface, hot pain like a blister and it isn't the pulsing of a tired, overused muscle. It isn't like the hammering pain of toes crunched up into a boot toe on a downhill haul. And it isn't the sharp needle pain of a pinched nerve either.

Rather, it feels like a railroad spike driven through your arch. After miles and days of this special kind of foot pain, "the feet," according to Marmot, " start to ache." Boots, if they haven't fallen apart by now, simply give up the ghost.

Not only do the feet take such abuse; the ankles get their share as hikers pick their way up the Trail. Step on this rock and the ankle bows to the right. Step on that rock and the ankles bows inside to the left. Stretch to step on what looks like a flat rock only to find that it rocks backward. It's hard to believe that an ankle can swivel so much. Stop for a moment to catch your balance, then step ahead, only to find that—thunk!—you didn't pick up your foot high enough and now you've hit a rock hard enough to send the vibration clear up to your knee. What feet and ankles don't absorb, the hip joints do as the hiker struggles to maintain balance.

Hikers try to keep a happy attitude about the rocks, because as Accorn pointed out, "you might as well, we're going over them anyway." Others decided to entertain hikers behind them by creating little contests in the Trail registers using rocks as part of the game. Gumby decided to challenge others hikers with his list of Pennsylvania's greatest hits, which included "Rock me, Amadeus," "Like a Rolling Stone," and "Rock Around the Clock." And Allgood reminded upcoming thru-hikers that complaining is not what hiking the Trail is about: "I have truly loved this beautiful state . . . If I wanted to read a bunch of bitching, I'd have gotten a newspaper editorial from New York, not a shelter register." A Wink and A Smile noted that they "met a nice woman who gave us some boiled water. She lives near Lehigh Gap, so I asked if the Trail up ahead is rocky, and she replied, 'Is this Pennsylvania?' "

Trail maintainers have the last word on the rocks, though, and true to hiker humor it's clever, understated, and clear. On many occasions the familiar 2 x 6 white blaze isn't painted on a tree at all. No, it's painted on the sharp edge of a rock lying half-buried in the Trail. And after all, why not? That's exactly where the hikers are looking as they pick their way through the second half of Pennsylvania.

By the time thru-hikers reach the Delaware Water Gap, Mikail Baryshnikov has *nothing* whatsoever over on them. If they've survived the 150-plus miles of rocks with packs on their backs, then by the time they come down the cliffs from Mount Minsi they have all of the muscle coordination that professional dancers have and are nearly as graceful, and all of this with packs on their backs. Which is good, because hikers have to make their way down from Winona Cliffs. If you couldn't see across the Delaware River to the great steel gray band of rocks on the other side in New Jersey, you'd swear that this is where the world drops off, so steep is the footpath down.

Rocks were not the only gifts Nature sent. Pennsylvania grew hot as the June sun bore down upon the hikers. To beat the heat, hikers started leaving early in the morning to take advantage of the cool morning air. During the month there were torrential rains from thunderstorms and that wonderful summer vine, poison ivy, appeared. Evidently by the time she reached the 501 shelter, Sprout had had enough of it. "I want some *more* poison ivy." Pressing North, not so lucky, noted, "Pennsylvania is passing fast and the poison ivy is coming out. My feet hurt and I have itchy spots. Have got to get some cortisone cream in town fast." Because of the storms, hikers in Pennsylvania found that picking their way over the rocks was tougher than ever. Further south, near Roanoke, Virginia, Ranger Dave, Annapurna and Woody Pop contended with flash flooding.

Hikers also continued to meet Ward Leonard. In Boiling Springs, H noted he'd "finally met Ward." Let It Be noted that he'd "finally met Ward, too." Sometimes the meetings were not always neutral, as Marmot and Allgood learned one night. "We were all asleep in the Darlington Shelter. I mean, we were out. And it was a full shelter. Out of nowhere, in the middle of the night, this guy walks up and starts shouting at the top of his lungs. 'These are my woods. I have a message for you punks. If you're in these woods, you're messing with me!' We all bolted awake and just sat there in our bags blinking at each other, wondering what in the world was that?" Other hikers had similar experiences, though most hikers pointed out that Ward seemed harmless enough. Other hikers weren't so sure.

On June 21 hikers up and down the Trail had the chance to participate in Nekkid Hiking Day. To celebrate the summer solstice, some say, and to add in a wacky way to the Trail experience, others say, and to break the boredom, a few say, some hikers hike 'nekkid' during the daylight hours of June 21. How many hikers actually did it, nobody knows, but at least one hiker, FAS, was caught in the act and reported—in Shenandoah National Park, of all places. As he made his way from Lewis Mountain, complete with the many road crossings, FAS crossed paths with a scout troop, which wouldn't have been so bad, except that there were a few scout mothers out walking with their sons, and they were mightily offended. Later that evening a ranger—thru-hikers figured that whoever was the low man on the totem pole was the one who got the nod—was sent out to chastise and admonish them.

"Any of you fellows know of anybody hiking naked?"

"No, we don't think we know about that."

"Are you sure you fellows don't know of anybody who was out here hiking naked?"

"No, no, we don't think we know of anything like that."

So it went until the hikers finally relented, owned up to their special crime, and promised never, ever, to do it again—especially when disapproving Scout mothers might be near by.

To add to the '96 experience, hikers enjoyed another phenomenon that only the 129 thru-hikers in 1979 and 1 thru-hiker in 1962 had enjoyed before them: The appearance of the 17-year cicadas. From the middle of Pennsylvania on down into Virginia, hikers were surrounded by the high-pitched, deafening drone of these monstrous insects. Shaped like a huge fly, the 17-year locusts are distinctive with their black bodies, gold colored wings, and bulging red eyes rimmed with gold. All day long the locusts were awakening, mating, reproducing, and dying. It was an awesome spectacle, one that wouldn't be repeated until the year 2013. After listening to the bugs drone on and on and on, Blueberry's response, typical of how many hikers felt, was "Shaaaddduuppp!" In Pennsylvania Sun Dog had the same reaction. "Cicadas everywhere! Ahhhhhhhhrrrhhhgh!" The Canadian Geese, however, assumed a philosophical, but nonetheless hiker, stance about the experience: "You wonder about the single mindedness of these cicadas, oblivious to all but the *single* goal of mating. Good thing we humans lead a more *balanced* life—Katahdin or death!"

Despite murder and depression, nekkid hiking and locusts, June closed out the month with a romantic gift: a blue moon rose on June 30 over the hikers, the only one appearing in the summertime until July 2004.

j u l y

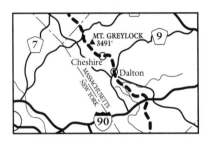

IT'S NO LONGER *IF* WE GET TO KATAHDIN,
IT'S *WHEN.*

-Sandman

What is July to the rest of America? An afternoon picnic? Wearing sandals? Eating ice cream before it drips down the side of a sugar cone? A week-long vacation at the beach? A furnace of a day that makes people walk quickly to the next dark and air-conditioned room?

To Appalachian Trail thru-hikers, July is when, suddenly, the hike changes tempo. No longer lulled into a sense of endless summer by the long summer days and the music of crickets, thru-hikers begin to feel the pull of Katahdin. They can't see it, and they can't touch it, and they can't taste it, but they can feel it, feel it in their bones. The magnetic pull of Katahdin, already wrapped around their hearts, eases into their brains, quickens their boot steps. The rest of the country might be slowing down to swelter in the heat, baking and roasting and perhaps even swearing as the dog days pass by, but not the thru-hikers. Katahdin pulls them northward like a magnet.

July began on a stormy note. Up in Massachusetts where Gutsy was putting in big mileage days to reach Dalton to pick up her mail drop, the rain made the hiking tough. "A thunder and lightning storm broke out on my way up East Mountain, but there was nothing I could do but keep going or be caught out in the dark. I had to put in almost 25 miles in order to make it to the post office." Hikers who had reached serene and peaceful Graymoor monastery in New York were, as Scout noted, glad for the roof over their heads "on such a treacherous night." Bloody Nose, breaking in his new boots on his way across New Jersey ("my others completely blew out, mainly from the Pennsylvania rocks") noted that Ole Swamper and Grasshopper were staying close behind.

By the time the country celebrated Independence Day, the weather had turned absolutely gorgeous; a breezy Canadian high pressure system had moved over the east coast. Poly + Ester celebrated July 4th in a typically creative hiker style. "Fireworks tonight . . . we're all getting together our MSRs, hoisting them up (while lit) into the trees and then throwing some burning twigs at them (dry ones that I've been saving in my pack). Then we're all singing *Goodnight Saigon* and *Hope I'm Standing Under the Mistletoe*. That's a celebration!" A Wink and A Smile noted that as they stopped for the night, they "probably wouldn't see any fireworks, though . . . If we have beans in our meal, that will be fireworks enough." At Graymoor, Wildhair took a few days off to visit with his wife and daughters, and start breaking in another new pair of boots—his third. "I guess I needed that!" he remarked. H stuck around the friary and enjoyed a bar-be-que with the monks. Goatman probably had the best seat on the Trail for fireworks. From Bear Mountain summit he "could see over 20 separate shows." Morning Glory tried her hand at polishing off a half-gallon of chocolate ice cream at the halfway point in Pine Grove Furnace State Park. She started eating it at 4 P.M. and finished about 50 minutes later. She didn't feel too badly, but "I had to wait an hour or so before I could order my cheeseburger. I skipped the fries." Further south, Mr. Bean took a little time off from the Trail to visit Gettysburg and the Amish country with his wife.

Sneakers stayed on the Trail, and was greeted with Trail Magic. "I was eating the remnants of some black raspberries going up the steep climb to Bald Mountain. The view from the top was worth everything: 360 degree view of all the mountains, farms and fields below. At Hog-Pen Gap, I got a ride down to the Spring from a guy from Richmond. He gave me a banana and some Tic-tacs. When I got back to the gap, Audrey Taylor showed up with a Pepsi. He comes up nearly every day to meet hikers. After another mile or two I found the Williams' goodie tree with water, crackers, and candy. As I was leaving the Williams' tree, a van with the Williams Trail angels pulled up. They gave me some still warm potato wedges, another coke and some more snacks. They're incredible. What a day."

Way down south on a section hike, Grim wondered if an American armada had turned out for him. "After hiking in the blazing sun all day, I came to the top of Watauga Dam and saw a long line of boats. Not just regular boats, but all overly decorated in red, white, and blue balloons, flags, banners. Since I was the only person on the dam, it appeared to be a parade in my honor, So I stood on top of the dam waving and yelling to all of the boats going by. There must have been at least 200. Quite exciting! It quickened my pace the rest of the day."

The hikers kept pushing north, enjoying the rhythm of their hikes. The Hiking Vikings took

Turdle and Gumby leave the Doyle.
Duncannon, Pennsylvania.

a day off in Port Clinton to visit the local Yuengling Brewery in Pottstown and devoured "half-a-cow cheeseburgers and a huge bowl of ice cream, thanks to Helen at the Port Clinton Hotel." Bungalow Bill and Contrary Mary, the Wonder Twins, prepared to dance with the Pennsylvania rocks, Plimsoul took in the ambiance at Duncannon and Da' Doyle, and Sweet Dreams passed the halfway mark. It looked like the hikers were set to make summertime miles. For sure all of the hikers marveled at the generous covered dish supper held at the Presbyterian Church of the Mountain. Exclaimed Cajun C, "They had everything! You should have seen the dessert table. I just wanted to take a picture of it and look at it up on the Trail when I really needed it!" Geo's hiking buddies gave him a birthday party at Spruce Peak shelter. Gutsy helped him celebrate the occasion and noted that his friends had hiked two miles in to reach the shelter, toting an incredible feast. "There was so much food I think I committed the sin of gluttony: steak, chicken, hot dogs, baked potatoes, salad, desserts . . . and more."

By mid-July, however, Mother Nature had decided to have a little sport with the hikers, for it would never do to allow the hikers think that they'd put *all* of the weather obstacles behind them. According to weather records, hurricanes are possible though highly unlikely to appear in July. So, sporting spirit that she is, Mother Nature sent one anyway, breaking a 100-year-old record to do so. Hurricane Bertha came raging through during the 13th and 14th, drenching the hikers with anywhere from four to five inches of rain.

Some hikers took cover wherever they could find it. Bonnie and Clyde called Bonnie's parents, who live close to Peter's Mountain in Pennsylvania, with an emphatic "Come Get Us Now!" Mr. Bean and Merlin stayed in Slatington, Pennsylvania, for the duration. Robohiker convinced hikers he was with to press on to reach the pavilion in Port Clinton. The roof there would provide some shelter. Wanderlust and Gray Rabbit stayed an extra day at the Mohican Center in New Jersey. Walk with Wong chose to strike out in the storm after his stay at the Mohican Center, leaving his current hiking partners, Wanderlust and Gray Rabbit behind.

Doc and Cornhusker, having opted to keep walking, realized that their choice meant coming down Winona Cliff at the Delaware Water Gap during the full force of the storm. While many hikers stayed on in the hostel at the Presbyterian Church of the Mountain, the Hiking Vikings spent a day in their tent at campsite #2 near Sunfish Pond, listening to the pounding rain. The Mapper was grateful that "Graymoor was a haven in the storm." Likewise, The Canadian Geese were thankful for their day at Bascom Lodge, "Been lucky to spend the day inside (dry) instead of outside (very, very wet)."

H and Guinness were hiking just north of Great Barrington, Massachusetts, where the Trail was eventually closed for a few days. "The water on the Trail got deeper and deeper to a depth of over 7 feet at one stream that fed the Housatonic. We used a floating bog bridge as a ferry for our packs and for Guinness since he couldn't swim." A Wink and A

Smile sloshed their way up the Trail, even as it and several bridges between Jug End and South Egremont in Massachusetts were under knee-deep water.

As Bertha raged through during the night, Lazy Bones sought refuge at Riga Lean-to just before Sage's Ravine. When he arrived, the shelter, meant for nine, was full of camp counselors, 22 of them to be exact. None of them offered any shelter space and finally Lazy Bones suggested that their tarps, which were going unused, might be useful if strung up just outside the shelter, as if to extend it. He thought it might create a little dry space for him and his partner, Honky-Tonk. They gave it a try, but it didn't work. The tarp didn't hold through the night and Lazy Bones and Honky-Tonk just got wet. In the morning Lazy Bones decided to keep hiking and found that the Trail, near Mt. Everett in Connecticut, more resembled a waterfall than a footpath. Knee-deep water rushing by him, he could not see any step he took. On blind faith he kept hiking, hoping that each step would be solid. How he escaped a sprained ankle was any-body's good guess.

Other hikers kept sloshing along, the hikers in Maine taking the worst of it. Under normal circumstances, hiking the Appalachian Trail in Maine requires that hikers ford 11 streams. With the passage of Bertha, the hikers would attempt to ford raging torrents, some suitable for kayaking.

Glider, who was closing in on Katahdin, was at Pleasant Pond when Bertha hit. "It absolutely poured for 20 hours straight. Every small stream became a ford and the normal fords were all waist-chest high. Basically you have to swim the river when it's that high. Some people with Therma-rests were using them as surfboards/kickboards and essen-tially surfing across the river. I just put everything I needed to keep dry in garbage bags and swam across. I managed pretty well, although I did lose a hiking pole and my pack cover."

Even after Bertha departed, hikers struggled with the after effects. Sir Goober Peas and Aunt Jemima faced their first serious, post-Bertha ford, Orbeton Stream. The *Thru-hiker's Handbook* warned that it could be "treacherous after several days of heavy rain." "How would a hurricane figure into this?" wondered Sir Goober Peas.

"As we descended to the canyon, we could hear the roar of the water. The stream was high, well over its normal banks, and probably 35 feet across where it abruptly intersected the Trail. I prepared for the worst, waterproof-ing my pack as best I could. Here it was not a question of getting wet, but instead of more basic needs such as surviving with life and limb intact.

"I was sufficiently nervous from my inexperience in stream crossings that I wanted to try out the route I had selected without my pack. I quickly found that water up to your mid-thighs gets to your waist once you're in the middle of it. The biggest challenge seemed to be a 15 foot wide section of the swiftest current, right in the middle.

"Having made it once safely, I braced for the added awkwardness of crossing with my pack. Any minor slip would be amplified by the top-heavy load. About 10 feet out I slipped once, but caught myself.

"Adding to the physical force of the water and the slippery rocks was the visual blur of both, and I nearly lost my balance from dizziness. A picture of me would have revealed gritting teeth and a furrowed brow until I got across."

Most bog bridges were under water and those that weren't were doubly slippery: oh what fun with a top-heavy pack! Large sections of the Trail were underwater. Glider "hiked for several hundred yards with the Trail under a foot of water the entire time."

Sir Goober Peas and Aunt Jemima had originally thought some southbounders were just talking junk when they claimed that their hardest stream ford was "the AT." One evening just before arriving in Monson, Maine, however, Sir Goober Peas and Aunt Jemima saw a small lake, through which the AT seemed to lead.

"A second look revealed an old beaver pond in the small valley, extending far in both directions. The water looked deep, and who knows how deep the muck was on the pond bottom. The usual tactic of seeking the path of least resistance led me back south on the AT. From the shore, it looked like I could make my way across this narrower section, perhaps by jumping from beaver flow to beaver flow. After all, if young trees were sprouting up on them they must be fairly sturdy.

"I made my way out a little, still dry. Before long I came to a spot where there was no connecting log or clump of vegetation. Cursing the state, the rain, and the lateness of the hour, I plunged in, finding myself only waist deep, not knowing really where to take my next step.

"Because I hesitated, the rotting vegetation below the water released a belch of methane that filled my nostrils. In addition to the stench, I was now faced with 100 or so yards of bushwhacking through a dense stand of young evergreens. Avoiding an eyepoking branch or hidden crevice made for slowgoing. Oh yeah, the trees were soaking wet, as if I weren't already.

"AJ tried the log rolling method, seeking as many stable logs going directly across where the AT 'led.' A couple of times he came to the last one and stopped, then finally took the plunge. Fortunately the muck and water levels were not as deep as he feared, and this probably proved to be the easiest way to 'ford' the AT. AJ reported no problems with his emissions."

The only hikers not really affected by Bertha were those who were further south, somewhat west of the path of the storm. They experienced cloudy days and some light rain, but nothing like what the northernmost hikers experienced.

Bertha finished her sport, and skies cleared. Monkey Butt, who had reached the White Mountains National Forest, thought that each day "might be the most beautiful on the Trail." Upon seeing the pamphlets for conducting a self-guided nature walk, other hikers, like Accorn, joked about continuing their own "self-guided nature walks."

As hikers in the Whites chugged northward, however, they had to deal with a freakish, post-Bertha windstorm. On July 20, winds across the Presidential Range maxed out at 153 miles per hour. "I was at Kinsman the day it hit," recalled Nomad, "so I was pretty lucky. I know a bunch of people who were pinned down in Lakes of the Clouds hut for a couple of days. As I crossed Lafayette, the winds were 80–90 miles per hour. Hiking the trail was a challenge at times because the crews had not been out since the day before to clear the Trail. We ended up doing a fair bit of trail maintenance that day just to make progress. It was neat seeing all of those big trees toppled over. It reminded me of a metaphor for life, something about the tallest trees feeling the winds the strongest and falling over."

Despite enduring what seemed like constant storms, hikers still found Trail life enjoyable. Buzz, coming through Pine Grove Furnace, did manage to eat his way through 2.5 gallons of ice cream, probably setting the record for 1996.

Throughout July, the main wave of hikers passed through the Trailside Zoo in New York. Ironically the zoo, the lowest point of elevation on the Trail, is also one of the most depressing sights for many hikers. There the trees are labeled and the bears, foxes, and coyotes, the same animals hikers have been living with for several months in a generally respectful way, are caged and pacing. Trail registers contained the hikers' reactions. At Graymoor, Allgood wrote, "Today was a little depressing. I took a walk through the Trailside Zoo with Erwin. We saw a bobcat and a coyote in cages no bigger than our tent, and we were both saddened by this. Then some bears and an otter who climbed to the top of his cage closest to me said "please won't the two of you take me out to the AT . . . I guess a zoo is a double-edged sword." Marmot was likewise disturbed, "Today was the first time I have walked through a zoo and felt like one of the exhibits." Craigmont later responded by writing, "I can feel a big register argument coming on. About the zoo thing. Sure . . . these inner city people should see wildlife, but maybe it would be more realistic if they took a walk in the woods. Seeing sickly animals locked up in cages as noisy people scream and yell is not my idea of a positive experience for the people or the animals."

Hikers were likewise forced to consider another facet of civilization: the real and continuing disappearance of wilderness lands. As hikers enjoy the Trail, they are often lulled into thinking that the wilderness in which they feel so peaceful is infinite. Indeed, at eye level and 2.5 miles an hour, it seems to stretch forever. Observed H, "Even when I'm at my fastest out here, I'm slower than everybody else." However, aerial observation of the Appalachian Trail clearly illustrates how fallacious that thinking is. Many times the Trail follows ridge tops. Everywhere, development pushes the edge. As the Trail goes into the northeast, the number of road crossings increases and hikers find that their wilderness sanctuary is more fragile than they imagined. In 1996 hikers learned that some Trail lands were in jeopardy of being lost forever. From the New Jersey state line to Orange Turnpike, 17,500 acres of land owned by the Sterling Forest Corporation were considered for use as housing for 30,000 people and for building 8 million square feet of office space. Hikers immediately saw another case of "pave paradise and put up a parking lot." Ranger Dave happened upon a zoologist further south in Manassas Gap. "He told me that the song bird population has been cut in half over the last 30 years. It's because their habitat is disappearing." He paused and then continued, "You don't want to admit that Rachel Carson is still right."

Farther north, hikers were struggling with fatigue and disease. For Gutsy, who had sent her stove home in an effort to lessen pack weight, the "months of mediocre nutrition are telling. I missed the stove more than I thought. It's difficult to plan filling meals without it." But starving wasn't the only problem she encountered. Making her way into Vermont, Gutsy very nearly didn't make it out of the state. After developing an angry sore on her leg and trying to treat it herself, Gutsy hobbled to a doctor in Manchester Center with the help of David, the caretaker at Peru Peak shelter, and a man who gave her a ride into town. Unable to walk at all and still nauseated, Gutsy lost a week of hiking while there.

The leg hurt so badly that she had to scoot on her behind to even reach the bathroom. Deciding to return to the Trail, but still feeling lousy, Gutsy tried to make miles. She did, but for a price. Limping and sick and sporting a big red ring on her leg and unable, even, to put on her boots, she went to the hospital in Hanover, New Hampshire, nearly 100 miles further up the Trail. The diagnosis? Lyme disease. Another hiker, Foghorn, was also suffering in the hospital with Lyme disease. Hiking Viking Rita brushed up against poison ivy somewhere in New Jersey and developed such a case of it that she was taken to the Sussex county hospital in an ambulance. The guys at the fire station in Unionville saw to that.

Walks there a thru-hiker who doesn't wonder if the whole thing, this state called Maine and this park called Baxter and this mountain called Katahdin, is a hoax? That maybe none of it exists? That maybe it's just a cruel joke meant to make your back ache and your knees throb?

For 75 miles in Georgia, for 375 miles in North Carolina and Tennessee, for 540 miles in Virginia, for nine miles in West Virginia, for 40 miles in Maryland, for 231 miles in Pennsylvania, for 163 miles in New Jersey and New York, for 141 miles in Connecticut and Massachusetts, they plod northward, trusting that they'll reach this Katahdin. They've seen pictures in books and magazines and L.L. Bean catalogs, haven't they? It is real, isn't it? Isn't it?

But for many months and many miles Katahdin is elusive. It plays cat-and-mouse with the hikers. Although reaching the mountain is the goal, hikers don't permit themselves to think too much about it. They can't. It's too much of a luxury. There's too much difficult ground yet to cover—the Green Mountains of Vermont and the White Mountains of New Hampshire lie ahead, as do 275 miles of the Maine woods. There's too much opportunity for injury or illness from giardia or Lyme disease or some other kind of Trail crud. There's too big of a psychic need to meet smaller, more immediate goals. Wanderlust noted the need for smaller goals, saying, "You have to have a carrot to get up the Trail. It's a long way to Maine. Even if your first carrot is to just make your way to Blood Mountain, you have to have a carrot."

Many hikers, such as Allgood, credit their ability to stay on the Trail by thinking *only* of smaller goals. Sitting in Port Clinton, Allgood remarked "When I was in Georgia, I reminded myself that I had never seen the

Smokies. So the Smokies became the goal. Once I reached the Smokies, I told myself that seeing Damascus would be the next goal. I had never been to Damascus. Once I reached Damascus, I decided that Troutville would be my next goal. From Troutville, the goal was Harper's Ferry. Now the goal is the Delaware Water Gap. After that, when I reach New York, I'm going to take a few days off, since I'm from New York. Then I'll be back on the Trail, ready to push to Katahdin. But I'm looking forward to the Whites, too." Gumby seconded the technique, saying, "You've got to be goal-driven. You have no choice but to have goals if you're going to make it to Katahdin. It doesn't matter if your goal is getting to the next post office or getting to the next shelter. The Trail says, 'Here, take this,' and you do. Having goals is the way you work with the Trail."

Hikers who cultivate an interest in the Appalachian Trail over and above making miles seem better able to set the small goals so necessary in getting themselves to Katahdin. Indeed, the Appalachian Trail is a living, breathing, challenging, outdoor classroom, more powerful in its impact than any textbook could ever be. Whatever natural and social lessons the hiker chooses to learn, the Trail can teach them.

The first lesson is forecasting the weather. Hikers become adept at reading clouds and breezes and are able to sense when the weather is changing. They may never know a cirrus cloud from a cumulus cloud, but they can tell you as the humidity rises or as a front is coming to bring rain. Hikers also profit from the regional lessons in weather. Northeastern hikers learn that the South can host severe winter weather. Southern hikers learn a few lessons about oppressive heat and humidity as they walk on the rocky ridges of Pennsylvania and by the sod farms of New Jersey. Hikers from west of the Mississippi learn about the effects of humid, wet air from the Gulf of Mexico. And every hiker stepping carefully on the barren tops of the Presidential Range of the White Mountains in New Hampshire learns how the three typical weather patterns on the eastern seaboard collide atop Mount Washington to bring about some of the consistently worst weather in the country.

The Appalachian Trail also teaches its students about geography and geology. As hikers pull up the peaks and push into the gaps of the Appalachian backbone, they tread upon ground that may be as much as a billion years old. Mica sparkles in the rocks, and weathered oxide deposits blush the rocks a faint orange. Hikers peer down, down into deep gorges and descend to broad rivers. They cross many balds of the southern Appalachians. They wind through boulder-strewn meadows, speed across near-level Pennsylvania farmland, and pick their way over rocks left behind from glaciers that disappeared over 15,000 years ago. They can stand upon the ridge tops and marvel at the wide swath that the Hudson River cuts across New York and wonder what view of a pristine America Henry Hudson beheld when he first sailed up this magnificent river in 1609. They pass numerous glacial ponds and walk against the wind above treeline in New Hampshire. They see at ground level the network of logging roads in Maine.

There is man-made history to contemplate as the hikers walk north. The Trail starts near the site of America's first gold rush—at Blood Mountain, Georgia, there are caves that supposedly hide Indian gold— and winds its way across pioneer homesteads, Revolutionary War battlefields, land traversed by Daniel Boone, Civil War battlefields, factories that have since disappeared, coal routes, canal ports, and old stage roads. Monuments decorate the Trail, some are to famous people, like the War Correspondents Arch in Gathland State Park in Maryland and some are to a way of life that has long since passed, such as the wrought iron Waterville Bridge now tucked across Swatara Creek. Structures like the Ironmasters Hostel, with its Underground Railroad tunnels, give hikers pause. Peering into the darkness of the escape routes makes their freedom that much more precious. K-Posa, hearing the noise from a factory near Tinker Cliffs realized that Benton MacKaye's vision of an Appalachian Trail was good. Any hiker, after having descended into and then back out of Harper's Ferry and passed the fortifications used by the warring Yankee and Confederate armies, has to appreciate the dedication that both sides demonstrated in carrying out their mission. Such terrain, difficult enough for hikers to traverse, would have been even more so for men who were expected to haul cannons, make miles and still go into battle. Any hiker, after having smelled the coal in Port Clinton, would better understand the sacrifices coal miners made to help build industrial America.

Hiking couples learn a few unique lessons of their own. For some, the experience deepens their bond. Matt and Tracey found that "throughout our journey we've learned about the Trail, our wonderful natural resources and beauty, and the intense kindness and surprise of Trail Magic. But most importantly we've learned about ourselves and our relationship with each other. The AT has given us the environment to build a stronger bond without the added variables . . . we've had time to stop to admire the flowers of spring and the butterflies of summer. But we've also hurried frantically to the next shelter in a violent thunderstorm."

Whatever lessons the hiker learns, it is a given that he or she will be exposed to the solitary and sometime painful lessons of mental discipline. On the AT they are served up in big helpings. Reaching Graymoor, Jester noted, "The AT mental toughness game has started for many of us. I continue day by day and many times it's a struggle." All hikers—purists, blue-blazers, slackpackers, and occasional yellow-blazers alike—must learn to manage all of the distractions associated with hiking the Trail.

First, just because hikers are in the woods doesn't mean that the lives they come from have stopped. Far from it. Often they must leave the Trail for a few days to attend weddings or graduations. H started hiking in early March, but had to return to his university for his own graduation. (Although he wore a tie with his cap and gown, he did decide to wear his hiking boots to the ceremony.) Occasionally hikers must take a momentary break to attend to family emergencies: Nexmo's father's surgery, Mr. Maine's aunt's funeral. Sometimes hikers leave to visit a place that's relatively close by. Screamin Knees and Cajun C took a break to go into New York City from the Delaware Water Gap, and other hikers opt to visit DC from Harper's Ferry. Sometimes the side trips are quite extensive, like when Chomp Cat and a friend opted to hitchhike from Tennessee to see the Atlantic Ocean. Q-Tip, Wookie, and Zoo took numerous breaks from their hikes, on one occasion to travel to New York to see the Phish concert. Sometimes a Trail town emits a siren call of extra days of indulgence. Whatever the cause for the momentary break, all hikers face a difficult choice: do they go back and resume a hiking rhythm or do they call it quits?

Sometimes the distraction is love. On the Trail, away from the grind of modern life, hikers often feel more open and comfortable with themselves and others. The result is that some hikers fall in love. When that happens, completing the Trail pales in importance, as Roses discovered. "I made it all the way to Vermont where I finally couldn't take it anymore. Rain, bugs, mud, and the same old food day in and day out takes its toll. Now I'm taking a vacation from my vacation. I'm driving across the country with another hiker I met . . . After I met her and fell in love, the Trail didn't seem as important anymore. Katahdin was no longer my first love, and after that happened, I lost all resolve. Then every little thing that went wrong was just another reason why I didn't want to hike. Thankfully she loves me enough that she left the Trail with me and we're on our way to California."

Occasionally the distraction comes from home. If spouses or parents didn't support the hike in the first place, phone calls home become litanies, urging the hiker to come home. "You've done enough," they say, "I'll love you even if you don't finish the Trail." Lucky hikers are those whose family and friends who arrange to meet them along the way, continuing to support the hiker. In Neels Gap, Attitude knew that his wife would meet him in Shenandoah, Wildhair's wife Dele met him in Damascus and then later in Harrisburg and then again in New York. Big Jim's wife walked sections with her husband, as did Gutsy's husband. Julie McCoy took time off to re-hike a section of the Trail with some friends. Quite often, couples start hiking together but one will decide to leave the Trail while the other prefers to stay. In those cases, the one who leaves often becomes the slackpacking assistant to the spouse on the Trail. Mrs. Honeymooner assumed this role when her knees cried "Stop!"

And others, like Cub, despite coming so far, suffer self doubt brought on by the uninvited critiques delivered by their fellow hikers. "Since I began, almost everyone I meet feels the need to tell me I will not make it to Katahdin. Some people actually come out and say, 'You'll never make it.' This is really beginning to drive me nuts. Are these people AT thru-hiking experts? Have they ever gotten off their ice cream eating asses and tried to walk 2,100-plus miles? Despite what they say in the movies, having everyone tell you 'you can't' is not inspiring. Perhaps they are right. Perhaps the weather will stop me in early October in New Hampshire or Vermont, but so what? For me this is not about Katahdin. I wanted to challenge my mind and my body. Would walking for five and a half months and 1,800 miles make me a failure?"

Other hikers wage war upon themselves because they are at once unable to develop the muley single-mindedness it takes to stay on the Trail and unable to leave it. Allgood reflected upon the internal conflict, saying, "Some people don't want to be here. And if they really don't want to be here, they should leave. It's just a lot of negative energy used up for nothing." Craigmont commented on that danger of even permitting himself to think about leaving the Trail, saying, "I remember being really, really exhausted. But after a while, you get used to being tired and bruised and smelly. But once you start thinking about getting off the Trail, you can hang it up. It [completing a thru-hike] ain't gonna happen." Morning Glory, reflecting on the shift from merely physical struggle to the mental one echoed Craigmont's insight. "This part of the trip is more of a mental, psychological challenge now that the body is in trail-shape. It's sometimes a little harder to get up and strap that pack on and walk up and down over mountains, hills, and ridges and roads all day long." It's especially difficult when the one set of hiking clothes you have smells like overripe roadkill, the smell most hikers refer to when they speak of "toxic sock syndrome."

As hikers learn that mental toughness and the cheers from the support team are more important than gear, conversations about who has what gear simply dry up. It honestly doesn't matter any more. Nor do prescriptions on how a hiker should clothe himself. K-Posa and Sandman were among several hikers whose sweaty hiking shorts continued to cause monumental chafing problems. For them to get to Katahdin, something would have to change, and as the chafing problem showed no signs of stopping, and they didn't think they were going to quit sweating—it was summer and they were hiking for goodness sake—K-Posa and Sandman decided that for them at least, sarongs would do just fine, thank you. They considered it the best fashion statement on the Trail in '96, as did curious onlookers who saw them.

K-Posa's gerry-rigged pack, compliments of dental floss.

Shaking his head, Gumby laughed and noted, "You cannot make a line up and guess who'll make it based on gear. Gear doesn't mean anything. I was really intimidated at Springer. This guy had custom everything—poles, boots, pack.

I thought 'Wow, he's going to make it.' But he got off the Trail in Neels Gap. These other guys had never even been out before, and one of them couldn't even use his stove. I just knew he was going to starve. But they're only a week behind me." Craigmont had started sewing his pack together using dental floss, but finally had to buy a new pack. "Yeah, no one is going to believe me when I tell them I'm thru-hiking. Look at how clean my pack is." K-Posa, when asked about his gear, just smiled. "Everything about me except my feet is gerry-rigged." K-Posa wasn't lying: he'd lost so much weight that he'd had to use duct tape and dental floss to secure a second hip belt inside the one already on his bag. Other hikers, seeing their boot soles separate from the uppers, just wrap a little duct tape around the two pieces and keep on walking and hope that the second pair of boots arrives as planned. Firefly had her own challenges with boots. After switching to a new pair of boots at Pine Grove Furnace State Park, she found that the new ones were cutting into her feet. After some 30 miles, Firefly switched to her Tevas and walked the remaining 164 miles to Delaware Water Gap to pick up a third pair of boots.

In the class of '96, Skylark certainly could have won the mental toughness award, were one to be given. When at the Dogpatch Tavern her pack was stolen, it wasn't enough that she'd gone the distance with the Georgia cold, the Smokies overcrowding, the heat, the Virginia blues, the daily pounding on her feet. Accustomed to living out of her pack, Skylark had to face the reality that now her *home* was stolen. Not just robbed, but stolen. Reconciling herself to the theft was all the more difficult because inside her pack was her journal and undeveloped film from Trail Days. When she discovered the theft, she was left with few choices. "I could either sit in Delaware Water Gap or I could walk. Sandman let me mooch off of him for 75 miles until I could get my pack replaced. So I walked." For Skylark, quitting wasn't an option. Nor were her fellow hikers going to let it be.

Not all hikers, of course, agonize over their decision to leave the Trail. They know that they *have* hiked enough. They've hiked more than they ever thought they would. As these hikers leave the Trail, they leave proud—and more than a little amazed that they were able to log as many miles as they did. Often at Harper's Ferry these hikers trade the title "thru-hiker" for "big-chunk hiker." A thousand or so miles is certainly a big chunk of the Trail, in anybody's book. It's certainly more than many, many people would ever think about doing, let alone attempt.

In 1996, an estimated 1,250 hikers left Springer Mountain between February and mid-May to attempt a thru-hike. By the end of July, 528 had passed through Harper's Ferry. As the thousand or so of would-be thru-hikers dwindle to the few hundreds, an interesting social order develops on the Trail. As Ranger Dave noted, "hiking itself, what you do during the day, can be a very solitary pursuit. But in the afternoons and evenings when you come into a shelter, all of the rules change and the experience then becomes a highly social one." Wanderlust mused upon the social dynamics and smiled. "Maybe instead of a national scenic trail," he remarked, "the Appalachian Trail should be called a National Social Trail."

Shelter registers help create the social order. Often nothing more than a wirebound notebook with its cover and inside pages swollen and soft from humidity and use, the register makes a community out of people who may never meet each other. In a odd and wonderful way, it gives hikers, who are moving everyday, a sense of place, of rootedness, of family. Hikers who are ahead serve as older brothers and sisters, providing support and information for the ones who come behind. And hikers comment on just about everything. No topic is too sacred—or silly—to be discussed.

Since food—either thinking about it, eating it or recalling what one has eaten or wondering what someone else might eat— is so important to a hiker's ability to complete his hike, hikers often use the Trail registers to —surprise!—talk about food. Sometimes they debate the relative merits of junk food, specifically whether Little Debbie or Tasty Cakes has the superior product. According to Sprout, "Tasty Cakes rule." On other occasions, northbound hikers leave tips to southbound hikers on where to find the best junk food. Sundog, pleased with the selection at the US 52 store, noted that he "pigged out at the store on 52. Buy one, get one free danishes." Sometimes hikers will record the damage they wreak at a buffet. "We sought AYCE. We devoured AYCE. We gave them a run for the money." Lucky for the restaurateur the establishment went unnamed.

Sometimes a hiker will record a story about what happened in a particular shelter for other hikers' use or entertainment. Wayfaring Man, taken with the activity of a black snake at Kirkridge Shelter, wanted other hikers to watch for the snake's reappearance. "A 5 feet six inch black snake climbed the oak out to the left. It entered a squirrel nest about 35 feet up and caused quite a disturbance when the four or five squirrels that lived there came home in the evening due to a thunderstorm." When the black snake departed later, Wayfaring Man saw three bumps in the snake's body and reckoned that the baby squirrels had been devoured. Otter described his second attempt at nude hiking and shared the experience for those that followed. "I decided to try my luck at nude hiking again. I tucked my shorts into my hip belt in case I needed them. [Hearing some-one coming toward me,] I decided to put them on, but was surprised to see them not there (so was the person I met). I backtracked a mile or so and then I gave up. They're gone!" A few days later, Sun Dog contem-plated his upcoming visit with his parents. "I wonder if they'll claim me as their son if I still smell the way I do now." In the Allentown Shelter, Dre noted an upcoming athletic match. "In for lunch. Aim to arm wrestle Zuma." Zuma followed up, writing, "I won." At one shelter, Sweet Pea wrote that she and Blue Iggy "celebrated June by spraying our hair green." Coming by about three weeks later, Little John told hikers about spending time with some weekenders. "I think the weekenders were bummed to find us using the shelter . . . my flaming marshmallow trick really gave us that sense of "family" and "togetherness" that we needed."

Hikers use the registers to give themselves and each other pep talks. These verbal pinches help hikers realize that yes, they're really getting closer to Katahdin. They also cheer up other hikers who that might be mentally struggling. Pilgrim, recapping his progress in Morgan Stewart shelter, said, "In for the night. What a wonderful day to walk in the woods, felt good. Tomorrow Connecticut! I think we are two-thirds there by now!" The Bird, about to exit Pennsylvania, wrote "I made it. Pennsylvania will no longer be history in the making, but only history. To all behind, take care, nurse your wounds, and dust off your soul."

Sometimes they share practical information, like when Zuma cautioned others behind him to "watch that first step" off the pavilion in Port Clinton. "Dre almost ended his hiking career last night going to relieve himself."

Others like to share their insights with fellow hikers. Crash noted that "being from the South I had always heard that Northerners were, uh, unfriendly, to say the least, especially those in New York. Well, so far, the hospitality around here just blows the South away!" Sometimes their insights are philosophical. For Bandana Light, the Trail, like a diamond, kept giving him facets of life to ponder. "I believe so much of this is just about living. Even on bad days, you will see a pretty flower or meet a new friend. It's about living in the moment, enjoying it all. Existing among

Nature, realizing you are only a part of the larger whole. I still struggle with defining what's going on out here and perhaps if I define it too much I destroy it." Sometimes the insights are wry and self-quizzical. For other hikers who would follow, Snowman noted that he "got up at 9:00 A.M. Hiked 12 miles. Ate lunch at 1:00 P.M. Must walk longer. Must like it."

The registers also serve as the Trail art gallery as thru-hikers draw pictures to entertain those who follow. Landshark's picture of a shark accompanied every entry he made and H left a hiking bear. One hiker carried an ink pad and stamp to leave behind his boot prints, in green ink, of course.

Because hikers do not all keep the same pace, the Trail register provides a way for hikers to keep up with each other. Having earned some notoriety during their Trail Days performance, Breakin' Wind, who was ahead of Heavy Breather, wanted Heavy B to know about his attempt at a reprisal of *Hotel Appalachia*. "I tried to sing it at a karaoke bar/restaurant in Culvers Gap the other day, but I was an octave too high and off key—it just wasn't the same without you." Mr. Bean, worried that Scout and Seadog would leave the Trail, left notes to them to keep them interested in hiking the Trail. He was surprised and pleased when he reached Harper's Ferry that they had sent him a card letting him know they were still out there.

In a time when most people's lives have been pureed and homogenized into a pre-conceived and bland experience, Appalachian Trail thru-hikers create a community rich in individual expression, texture, empathy and caring. Monkey's Butt's twisted ankle cause many hikers to hold their breath. Said Gumby, "I had been reading Monkey Butt's entries and really enjoying them. But when I read that he had hurt his ankle and it looked like he was going to have to leave the Trail, I got all worried for him, and I don't even know the guy. But I know what he's been through and I worried about him."

As the numbers grow smaller, the bonds among those who remain grow tighter. They share a million things, some of them gross: the dank smell of shirts and shorts and gear that have been wet too long for too many times, boots that don't dry, knowing how gummy it feels to crawl inside a sleeping bag and try to sleep despite sticky arms and legs, eating mac and cheese *one* more time, and as Glider noted, "telling yourself that the squishy feeling inside your boot is really a foot massage." However, some of what they share is wonderful, like the feel of a freshly washed and fluffy sock, the amusement of standing in the rain fully clothed and washing themselves and their clothes at the same time, the sensory pleasure of eating freshly baked goods out of a mail drop. (Bloody Nose's mom became famous for the homemade brownies, cookies and gorp she sent her son. "She sends so much that I'm always giving some away," Bloody Nose said.)

That the hikers look inward to themselves for support and entertainment is nowhere more obvious than in their dislike of television. Turdle observed that "it's only death, weather and sports. It's always the same plot line, the same story. Nothing ever changes. You can tune in every six months and not miss much." K-Posa had a similar reaction, noting that when he did have access to a TV, "I see if I can find a nature program on the Discovery channel. Those other programs are way too intense." Several '96 hikers went to see *Independence Day*. Their defenses down and rusty, the hikers were overwhelmed by the special effects—in other words, the manipulation. "I've never had a movie affect me like that," said Marv of the Hiking Vikings.

They come also to dislike the "too muchness" of modern life. In grocery stores, for example, the lights are too bright, there's too much noise, people drive too fast, things smell too strong, especially the soap aisle. It unnerves many hikers and they find it difficult to find the right items. Shaking his head, K-Posa sighed and said, "All I wanted was creamy peanut butter, but I realized when I got out of the store that I had bought

Lemstar's party, attended by Pony Express, Han Solo, Home Brew, Cat in the Hat, Hiking Viking Marv, and others. Hessian Lake, New York.

crunchy. Another time I wanted Wheat Thins, but I later realized I had picked up the low salt kind. There were just too many things in there to see." Sandman had similar reactions. "Yeah, when we go into a grocery store, we keep making eye contact for safety. Those places are loud." Interestingly, so unaccustomed are the hikers to having to fight to make themselves heard—it's quiet out there in the woods—that even when they're in a group, they're incredibly soft-spoken. Blasted by boomboxes by the hordes at Hessian Lake the day of Lemstar's party, the Cat in the Hat just looked around shaking his head, saying "this is too much. Just too much." Many of the hikers remark that they can smell dayhikers long before they see them because of all of the cosmetics on them.

In many cases the social order the hikers create for themselves is positive and affirming. When Skylark discovered that her pack had been stolen, 27 hikers secretly planned a surprise birthday party for her in Boiling Springs, partly to cheer her and partly to re-outfit her. Mrs. Honeymooner drove 60 miles to pick up hikers to bring them to the party. On another occasion, Lemstar, a hiker from New York, had friends pull together a cookout at Hessian Lake for thru-hikers who were in the area at the time. However, the social order on the Trail can become negative. It is as if some hikers create the very things they despise in "the other world."

There is no guarantee that hikers will like each other, though the majority do develop a rare and deep bond, both with their current fellow hikers as well as thru-hikers from previous years. Cloaked in a Trail name, the hikers have an opportunity to be who they want to be without the trappings and signals of job, family, and home. Many of them assume a new persona, although over the course of the hike, their personalities do emerge, as Bad DNA, a 1994 thru-hiker, pointed out. "The stresses of the Trail highlight everything about you, both good and bad." OO7, a hiker from England, noticed the complex social dynamics and remarked, "When I first read about the Appalachian Trail, I thought it would be me and the Trail. When I got out here, I saw that it was me and the Trail and the pressing need to be, at times, a diplomat."

The age differences among the hikers are worked out early. When the hikers leave Springer, older ones tend to pooh-pooh younger hikers' perceived aimlessness. "They say they're out here looking for answers, but they haven't lived long enough to know what the questions are," say many of the retirees. Younger hikers, intent on delaying the chains of jobs and mortgages, don't go at their hikes as if they were jobs. In the spirit of Trail tolerance the groups reach an unspoken, albeit sometimes uneasy, truce. Many hikers noted that the Trail seemed to be attracting Dead Heads since Jerry Garcia's death had squelched their ability to follow the concert tours. Other hikers bemoaned the number of smokers on the Trail, saying that putting up with second-hand smoke wasn't something they had counted on. Occasionally hikers with dogs draw criticism when they couldn't stop their dog from barking or picking fights.

No social dynamic among hikers rouses the need for diplomacy more than what, exactly, constitutes a thru-hike. As hikers leave the Trail for one reason or another, the topic of how the remaining hikers are getting themselves to Katahdin generates strong opinions. Interestingly, many hikers come to the Appalachian Trail saying that they want to escape the ills of "society." But a minority create a highly competitive society on the Trail. It is so competitive sometimes that other hikers often refer to it as a "war."

On the surface, the definition of what constitutes a thru-hike is deceptively simple: a person attempts to hike from Springer Mountain, Georgia, to Mt. Katahdin, Maine, in a single season carrying a pack that, for the most part, contains just about everything a hiker needs to make the trip. Furthermore, the hiker must carry that pack past all of the white 2 x 6 inch blazes that mark the literal Trail. Whether the hikers chooses to start at Springer Mountain and hike north or start at Mt. Katahdin and hike south doesn't matter.

The hikers who actually complete a thru-hike of this sort are, however, few and far in between. For starters, few, if any, hikers spend every night on the Trail, either nestled in their tents at designated campsites or wedged in with others in the shelters built and maintained by the Appalachian Trail clubs. Most hikers spend only up to 10–12 consecutive nights actually on the Trail, away from commercial opportunities for sleeping and bathing. Quite often hikers take advantage of hostels built on or near the Trail, or motels or inns that they can reach by walking or hitchhiking, or perhaps of being taken to the home of a generous Trail Angel. That a thru-hike is not necessarily composed of four to six months of unwashed, forested solitude is a given and nobody gets too riled up about it.

Suppose, however, that the hiker hikes past most of the white blazes and occasionally takes a blue-blazed trail. Can the thru-hiker call him- or herself a thru-hiker? This is where the controversy—and need for diplomacy—starts. As Tarkus, a '92 thru-hiker described it, "After you've hiked either 30 or over a thousand miles, you begin to find that some of the strong convictions you had about how to 'do' the AT start getting a little fuzzy around the edges. As time goes by, sometimes you can have a real struggle with yourself."

Occasionally on the Trail, blue-blazed routes provide alternates that a hiker may choose to follow. Often the blue blazed trails point the way to a less difficult traverse, such as the Albert Mountain Bypass Trail in North Carolina or the bad weather route around Mt. Washington using Tuckerman's Ravine. For northbounders, Albert Mountain serves up the Trail's first significant, steep rock scramble. Likewise, Mt. Washington, some 1,725 miles north, is home to some of the worst weather in America and following the AT across the treeless Presidential Range can be dangerous if winds are blowing in excess of 40 miles an hour, which they often do, or if the summit is socked in with fog, making it nearly impossible to see the chest-high cairns that mark the Trail. Where the Trail crosses the Kennebec River in Maine, hikers must decide if they are strong enough to ford the currents of that river or take a nearby ferry across. If, however, a hiker makes a practice of always dodging the natural obstacles, can he or she really be called a thru-hiker? Some hikers, called "purists" by their fellow hikers, might answer "no"; hikers who are habitual "blue blazers" cannot also be "white blazers," or purists. Purists are sometimes so respectful of the white blazes and the spiritual journey they represent that they make it a point to pass each one. Some purists pat each one with a kiss as they walk by.

But what if a hiker does in fact walk past every white blaze, climb every mountain, and ford every river but does so without the pack? This practice, called "slackpacking" by the hiker community, means that while the hiker's feet literally carried him from Point A to Point B on the Trail, someone else took the pack in a vehicle from Point A to Point B for the hiker, thereby removing from the hiker the burden of carrying the pack and making the hike easier. Some purists say that this practice does not constitute a thru-hike, that only people who walk past every blaze *and* carry their packs can be called thru-hikers. However, because the percentage of people who slackpack substantially outnumbers those who don't, slackpackers are generally accepted as thru-hikers, even though some purists will disagree quickly.

(It should be added that slackpacking doesn't always make a day easier, as Q-Tip, Wookie, and Zoo learned. They were going to slackpack from Clarks Ferry to the Bleu Blaze Hostel, just over 32 miles. They didn't take much with them. "We didn't have anything with real calories in it," said Wookie. After a late start, they progressed 15 miles into the woods. Night fell and it began to rain. Harder and harder it rained, until they finally tried to curl up under a hemlock tree. "You just can't go too far on Sweet Tarts." At 3:30 A.M., cold, wet, and hungry, they got up and started stumbling along the Trail. "Finally we made it," said Q-Tip, but we were dead.")

Sometimes hikers start in spring with the crowds, but later decide to take an extended leave of absence from their hike. Even though they come back to the Trail to finish their splintered hike, picking up exactly where they left off and carrying their pack past every white blaze, does their journey constitute a thru-hike? It wasn't completed in a single attempt; it was *hikeus interruptus.*

And what about the "yellow blazers," the people who decide that hitchhiking most of their way to Katahdin is the best way to get there? Most hikers don't start out as yellow blazers, though each year a small minority of people come out more for the fun associated with hiking the Trail than with hiking the Trail itself. Having no intention of hiking, these tag-alongs may not even carry anything more than a simple day-pack, and may not even own boots. (There is no need, because, well, they aren't hiking.) In some cases, hikers with pets cannot follow the Trail, like in the Smokies for example. National park rules plainly state that, if a hiker has a pet, boarding arrangements must be made. Then because the hiker is unfamiliar with where the pet might be boarded or because a kennel fee is too pricey for the budgets, the hiker opts to yellow blaze around the Smokies. Some hikers fall into the practice of yellow blazing because fatigue exacts a real price but they want to stay in sync with their Trail partners. Other hikers discover that it's fun to show up at the next shelter ahead on the Trail and tease those who come walking up, sweaty, smelly, and tired, with a hearty "hey, what took you so long?" Yellow blazing thus provides a way to enjoy the Trail—and yet not hike—at the same time. Habitual yellow blazers, the hikers "who have blisters on their thumbs" from the air currents of passing vehicles, draw substantial criticism from the purists, blue-blazers, and slackpackers for this crime.

The spirit that gave birth to the Appalachian Trail did not aim to make hiking the Trail a competitive sport. The original argument made by Benton MacKaye, the gentleman credited with the idea of setting aside land for an Appalachian trail, was that the Trail should serve as a place of respite from the ills of a modern industrial and competitive society. Wingfoot, a 10-time thru-hiker and compiler of a popular reference book used by many hikers, recognized that as the number of thru-hikers increased, so would the undercurrent of competition. To that end, he cautions hikers to "hike your own hike." Many thru-hikers try to subscribe to that principle, realizing that there is nothing except ego-strokes to be gained in arguing about what really constitutes a thru-hike. (Using humor to deflect misplaced competition, they also generalize this wisdom to others activities: pitch your own tent, take your own pictures, treat your own water.) Neill Ross, thru-hiking in 1973 when shelters were fewer and farther apart and fewer side trails had been blue-blazed, remarked, "who is anyone to sit in judgment of anyone else? If you're having a good time, what do you care what other people think?" Jim Owen, a '92 thru-hiker, believes that thru-hiking is a microcosm of life itself. "One part of 'hiking my own hike' is knowing my own ground rules. It means writing my own contract and then living it. If you don't know what 'your hike' is how are you gonna know if you're hiking it?"

As the rest of the world sat near their televisions in air-conditioned comfort to watch the Olympics and curse NBC coverage, the edge of a blade-thin, smelly, hungry human bracelet stretching north from Virginia was about to find the magic clasp: Katahdin. Without fanfare, multi-million dollar endorsement agreements, parking problems, and wild applause, northbound hikers who had beaten the odds began their ascents to see that final white blaze. As southbound hikers crossed paths with the lucky northbounders, they brought reports that some hikers "made it." Faltering hiker resolve strengthened once again. Maybe Katahdin was for real, after all.

august

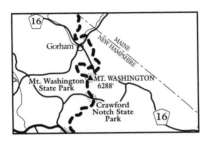

I HAD NO IDEA IT WOULD TURN OUT THIS WAY—
AND IT'S STILL NOT DONE TURNING OUT.

- B B

Whatat would August hold? If Katahdin and its mystical pull were real, if there really were one final white blaze upon a mountain top in Maine, could the thru-hikers still on the Trail traverse the remaining miles—and scale the final mountains—to find it? Even as a few hikers could call themselves "through," the majority were still behind.

And what about the Trail? Ever since the hikers had started passing from New Jersey into New York, they saw that the moderate roll of the mid-Atlantic states was building into a tougher, more serious terrain. Sure, Pennsylvania had its tough spots—many hikers just swore and shook their heads about the climb into and out of Lehigh Gap—but it wasn't anything they couldn't handle. They were strong and in their hiking prime, and covering ground was not generally a problem. And hikers who called New England home looked forward to the home turf of the Berkshires of Massachusetts and the Green Mountains of Vermont. The White Mountains of New Hampshire, however, loomed on the horizon.

Most thru-hikers look forward to traversing the Whites because they are ruggedly beautiful and unlike anything the northbounders have seen thus far. But the challenge of hiking in these mountains is unequaled by anything else on the Trail. As the green tunnel gives way to treeline, hikers find themselves surrounded only by rocks under their feet and by wind roaring against their faces. It's a landscape where the weather routinely conspires with the rocky terrain to teach a hiker, even the strongest hiker, a little humility. No matter how conditioned a hiker is, the hiker *will* slow down and pay proper respect to this grand landscape. Tradition holds that even when a hiker reaches the Whites and has put 80 percent of the miles behind, he or she still has 80 percent of the work ahead. It isn't easy picking your way up, over, down, and through 25 miles of boulders when you're carrying a 40-pound pack in wind that often exceeds 30 miles an hour.

The challenge of the terrain in turn posed the question of time. Was the time needed to complete the thru-hike running out? Even with all of the wonderful scenery to savor in August, the month is loaded with powerful signals that the idyllic life on the Trail will soon end. Hardwood trees whisper the changes. Their smaller leaves make woods and forests look more delicate and remind thru-hikers that a harsher, earlier winter holds court in this part of the world. Here and there in random spots, sparks of red and splashes of orange and drifts of yellow begin to hint that the green tunnel will soon change into a kaleidoscope of harvest colors. The growing frequency of green-fingered ski slopes tapering down the sides of nearby mountains signal that snow and ice will soon blanket the land. The sun climbs lower in the sky each day. The hikers must reach Katahdin soon, or quit because they have run out of time.

The late, wet spring and the abnormally wet July produced a bumper crop of biting, blood-sucking bugs in 1996. The swarms were expected to be so thick that even the evening news in Boston carried a feature story. The bugs had been bothersome since June, but as Bertha tore up the eastern seaboard and enhanced mosquito-breeding conditions, August began on an exceptionally buggy note. Black flies, mosquitoes, chiggers, ticks, no-see-ums, it didn't matter: All of the biting devils conspired to torture hikers, from New York to Maine.

It's difficult to appreciate the special torment flying vermin can deliver until you've grown dizzy from watching the insolent beasts swarm about your head, felt them crawling on your body looking for a place to bite, and then watched blood trickle down from the bite or a tiny whelp raise its itchy little head. Hikers try all manners of defense. First is mental discipline. Hikers will often try to tell themselves that the bloodsuckers are not a problem. They ask themselves how much can a mosquito bother them, really. It's only black flies for Pete's sake, not fractured heel bones and shin splints. Mental discipline has worked so often under so many circumstances before, why not now? They've talked themselves through bigger pains and discomforts before.

Sometimes they try wearing fine mesh jackets and pants that supposedly block the tiny devil from biting. But the bloodsuckers often just hang onto the mesh and bite anyway. As hikers swat and mash the trapped insects, they must then contend with wearing mesh that's spotted with dead bugs. Some hikers put on their cold weather gear—long Capilene underwear and long-sleeved shirts—and decide they can better take the heat and sweat and odor than they can hack the biting devils. Others, against their better judgment, buy bug dope that contains significant percentages of DEET and use it liberally. Damn the effects. It's the preservation of sanity we're talking here, when black flies join forces with mosquitoes and no-see-ums to make life miserable. Hikers who carried tents were glad for the trade-off with weight: At least they didn't have to sleep through the smack of shelter-mates slapping insects throughout the night.

It would be hard to know where the biting devils were the worst. Nomad fought his share in Maine, as did Gutsy. Cornhusker and Doc thought that the worst thicket was just before South Egremont, Massachusetts. Wildflower commented that "the flies and mosquitoes were really bad. They just swarmed in and around my ears. I couldn't

Doc and Cornhusker headed north to Crawford Notch, New Hampshire.

even take a break to sit down and eat a snack. And I was so hungry. Finally I just sat down and cried." FAS seconded the assessment. "The only way I knew to solve the problem was to keep walking. One afternoon I did 14 miles after 4 o'clock just to get away from them."

Walk with Wong slapped at mosquitoes furiously. "Finally I hurled my walking stick into the woods so that I could slap them with either hand. I thought, 'OK, come on. I'm ready for you now.' Because I didn't have anything else to think about, I decided to see how long it would take after I was bitten for the itch to subside. So I let a mosquito bite me and then I smacked him and then timed it. I found out that if I didn't scratch it for five minutes, the itch would go away." Greywolf and Caspar swatted at mosquitoes and, in a desperate dash down Prospect Mountain in Connecticut, ripped off nine miles in three hours trying to outdistance the bugs. "I'm from Savannah," noted Caspar, "I thought I knew about mosquitoes. But those black flies . . . now that was wicked." Just north of Graymoor, BB just cut to the chase in the war against the bugs. "I found some Yard Gard in a store today. It shall save my sanity." Probably all hikers agreed with Landshark's sentiment: "Why did God in His infinite wisdom, invent no-see-ums?" If God chose to answer, the Almighty would probably say, "to make sure thru-hikers really, really wanted to reach Katahdin."

Bugs aside, August was generally pleasant. Wildhair credited the better weather to his heaven-sent plea to "make it stop raining." He was nearly hypothermic in Franconia Notch and angry at the Appalachian Mountain Club members who wouldn't make room for him in the shelter at Garfield ridge. "'You should know what it's like to be wet,' they said." At the end of his resilience Wildhair offered up a his desperate plea. It must have worked because clear skies took control of the northeast and the hikers had a remarkable string of dry, beautiful days. Zipper, who had made his way to Massachusetts, noted that "it was great to finally see the sun again." Doc and Cornhusker were scared to count how many days in a row the skies had been clear. "I don't want to jinx it. I'm just glad to have a dry shirt," laughed Doc. Cornhusker was glad also, for a different reason. His boots were just about to fall apart and he preferred to limp into Gorham with dry feet rather than wet. When it did rain, some hikers were lucky enough to beat it. Landshark, finding shelter at Zealand Falls hut, noted that "it was close, but the Terminators beat the rain again. Hah!!"

View of Crawford Notch from Zealand Falls, New Hampshire.

Temperatures in the northeast were cool, in fact cold, at higher elevations. Hikers were beginning to need their cold weather gear again. Wildflower was particularly sad about having to switch over to winter gear. "I've been carrying a hammock and enjoying mid-day naps. But now that I've got to carry the heavier winter gear, I guess I've got to ship that hammock back home. I sure will miss it." Scamper and Rosy, picking up their winter gear near Dalton, bemoaned the weight, too. "Well, it's into town to pick up that heavy winter gear."

With better weather and sunny skies, hikers could focus on the good life of the Trail. FAS was privileged to meet the AT Stick Man, and after "finding the stick the AT Stick Man had left, I walked the next day to Cheshire and there was a carnival at a church. Father Tom grabbed me, gave me a couple of burgers, some corn and a beer. After the thing was over, we had a great time cleaning up the chairs and tables and finishing the leftovers."

Inching northward, many hikers found Bascom Lodge at Mt. Greylock to be a welcome respite. The highest point in Massachusetts, Mt. Greylock provides a wonderful view of the surrounding country side. Ranger Dave waxed eloquent about the area, saying, "I feel like I'm in

Switzerland. Awesome views. Awesome sunset. Awesome sunrise. Tre' magnifique! These are the treasures which come along." Many days throughout August, hikers were able to gaze across the interlocking ridges of the Berkshires, down upon the early morning clouds that settled on the towns below.

It also doesn't hurt the ambiance that the roofline of the rustic lodge resembles structures from 16th century England. The croo working there, incredibly mellow and warm to thru-hikers, earned lots of praise. Some hikers asked to exchange work for meals and a night's stay. Turbo paid them a special compliment saying that "croo magic makes me happier than Homer J. Simpson in an AYCE donut store." Lots of hikers, The Purple Pirate, Plimsoul, Scout, and Seadog among them, opted for

a shower and a meal on the porch before moving on. For Ajax, the shower at Bascom was the first shower he'd had since leaving Graymoor, some 180 miles back. H appreciated some leftover French toast he ate there, and The Cat in the Hat and Blueberry dined on leftovers, noting that "they were better than we get at home." FAS, Big Jim, and Wildflower thought that the huge calzones served up for their dinner were heavenly. The brownies baked by the kitchen staff were especially popular—some might say inspirational— as Annapurna experienced. "Face your emotional mountain—listen to the darkness fading to light— let the stone of your

*FAS washes windows in exchange for a night's stay.
Mt. Greylock, Massachusetts.*

inner child soften you! . . . Can't help myself—every once in a while I have to let this energy out! Enjoyed a nice break here—coffee talk with myself and a brownie with walnuts. Onward to Vermont!"

Vermont, however, presented a Janus face to the hikers. First the Vermont bugs greeted them, and then fatigue crept in. Like many hikers before him, Bloody Nose, a strong hiker, "began getting physically tired." He was not looking forward to New Hampshire and the Whites if things didn't improve. Allgood and Marmot considered leaving the Trail. It rained every day but one when they passed through, and they were so completely tired of walking in knee-deep water. On the other hand, Tom and Millie enjoyed Vermont. "Since Virginia it had been hard for me, but finally in Vermont I started to enjoy the hike again."

Other hikers didn't seem to notice Vermont, so focused were they on the Whites. To Wildhair, Vermont was simply "roots and mud. The Trail in Vermont sure takes a beating." Some who did take note of their surroundings saw severely overused, unimproved trails, and more than a few were outraged that they were having to pay to stay in shelters, especially when they couldn't tell that their fees were being reapplied to the sections of trail they were using. Others noted that hiker etiquette suffered. Nomad reported that many non-thru-hikers didn't subscribe to the practice that "the shelter isn't full until the last one is in." Bog bridges were rotten and disintegrating. Even porcupines were aggressive, as Calvin learned. One day on the Trail, a porky just lay face down, quills poised, refusing to move. Finally Calvin decided to back up, and take a running leap at the beast, yelling at him all of the way. The porky did waddle off, but was in no great hurry and wasn't really impressed, reported Calvin. The stretch after Killington, Vermont, into Hanover, New Hampshire, was boring, buggy, and muddy.

Most hikers did enjoy the hostel at Manchester Center, especially the availability of bar-b-que grill. H took part in a grill-out feast, complete with fresh corn. The Inn at Long Trail was another happy stop for hikers and many of them enjoyed the Irish folk music and Guinness Stout flowing at the bar. Hikers also took pleasure in the fact that the various hiking paces gave way to new combinations of partners. Remarked BB, "We've hooked up with two more women and a big hairy dog. It's great being a voting block of four women. Finally we outnumber the men in the shelters. It's a strange feeling to tip the testosterone balance for a change."

When hikers cross into New Hampshire, the first thing they meet is Hanover, certainly the most upscale Trail town there is. After months of passing through towns that are tremendously friendly but generally just a couple of clicks above scruffy, hikers are surprised by Hanover. Decorated with flower beds, wrought iron street lamps, and storefronts with awnings, Hanover is loaded with the self-aware charm of a New England college town, which it is. Dartmouth College sits on a wide expanse of green near the Trail and lends an academic air. For the hikers, however, Hanover is where they repair their tents and boots or buy new gear to replace what's falling apart.

In an outfitter's store, a new boot sitting under the lights is a virile item. The leather is sleek and burnished black or rust, the laces taut and clean, the soles fresh and glossy. Everything about it purrs power and muscle. But a dead or dying boot, which is what many hikers have when they reach Hanover, is pathos unlimited. On a dead or dying boot, the soles flop away from the uppers like the tongue of a miserable dog panting in August heat. The sides gape wide open, and little holes appear near the eyelets closest to the shoe break. The boot is the color of Trail mud, in all its variations. Too many footsteps, rocks, rain, and mud have exacted a toll. And hikers can ill-afford to have their feet flopping in the breeze as they cross the Whites.

The Whites do not disappoint, even though they are positively overrun with people because of the resort-like management. These magnificent mountains combine the grace of the Southern Appalachians with the raw, barren grandeur of the alpine areas of the Colorado Rockies. Below treeline, the red fruit of bunchberry and the blue-bead lily bearing its single, royal blue berry color the Trail. Above treeline, blackish rocks spotted green by lichens create a different landscape, one that resembles pictures of moonscapes. As thru-hikers emerge from among the stunted, twisted, wind-whipped spruce and fir trees—many of the trees more than 175 years old and still only chest high—and listen to the roar of wind as it rolls across the rugged landscape, they are enchanted by the landscape. The thin, grainy soil, the result of ancient oceans and the powerful scraping of glaciers, is so very, very different from the thick red clay custard of north Georgia where their hikes began.

The alpine landscape begins at Mt. Moosilauke, the western-most peak above 4,000 feet. For some hikers, Mt. Moosilauke is magical. "After being under the trees, I walked and I walked and pretty soon I could see the sky through the trees and then it wasn't long before I was above the trees and I could see everything. It was pure magic. The weather was just perfect!" exclaimed Cough Drop. "The hike is hard, but you go much slower and savor the views and the whole experience." Other hikers who climbed it in the clouds, like K-Posa and Sandman, found it to be wonderful too. The eerie, dreamlike beauty of being above the trees and yet in a cloud is unparalleled.

Chest-high cairns shaped like big rocky beehives mark the Trail when it is above treeline. Even if hikers have seen pictures of what the Trail looks like in the Whites, they are still amazed by how difficult the hiking is. Accustomed to clicking off 15 to 20 miles on an typical day, hikers are surprised by their slower pace. "Ten miles in 7.5 hours," noted Pilgrim. "This must be New Hampshire."

Looking at pictures doesn't reveal how big the rocks are and how carefully hikers must pick their steps through them to avoid injury, because photography plays a visual trick: It reduces a three-dimensional landscape to two. Plus it's not just a mile or two that the hikers must cross. Altogether about 16 miles are above treeline in the Whites. The ascents are steep and the descents plunge downward forever. Why not crawl down a vertical wall instead? Hikers with sore knees (everybody, right?) wonder if they will make it. Landshark, using humor to distract himself from the beating his knees were taking, laughed about his traverse through the Whites, calling it the "Climbing Pain Peak Tour." Hikers start measuring their progress in terms of time, not distance, as hiking turns into rock scrambling. Recovering and still tired from Lyme disease, Gutsy pulled herself into and out of Franconia Notch but was paying for it. "I was tired because the climbs over the rocks were forcing me to use all my reserves and when Dan tried to show me where Galehead Hut was—on a mountain in the far distance, still—I lost it and just began crying." Firefly did battle with Webster Cliffs, with its several false summits. "I thought I was never going to get there." Mr. Honeymooner was impressed with the way Mt. Washington took on a life of its own. "It was big from a distance and I could see where I was going to go, but the closer I came, the bigger the mountain grew. It just got bigger and bigger and bigger. Of course, when you get to the top of Washington and you're confused by all of the weather equipment and you're absolutely dogged out and still dying from the climb, you find that people can drive their cars up there. "

Nor would a photograph show the strength of the winds that whip across the summits. The White Mountains sit where three and occasionally four storm paths intersect. As a result, weather is so unpredictable that, even though there is a weather station on top of Mt. Washington, forecasters don't even attempt to predict the weather on the summits until the morning each day. Often wind comes out of nowhere blowing at near hurricane strength. In a wind blowing at least 40 miles an hour, he estimated, Mr. Honeymooner used both walking sticks to brace himself as he crossed the Presidentials.

Clouds pose a particular problem for hikers because when the clouds race by, the Trail simply disappears. Getting lost is all too easy. Clouds, however, add their own beauty to the landscape and many hikers enjoy watching the coral flame of a disappearing sun through blue-gray clouds. Probably the only disconcerting thing about the Whites is that as hikers near Mt. Washington, they must contend with the splinters and coal belched out from the train on the Mt. Washington Railway. Thru-hiker tradition, however, suggests that hikers bend over and moon the railway to retaliate for the smoke and cinders, and compensate for the climb.

On a clear day, however, the slow-going push is worth savoring. Tiny alpine flowers adorn the rocks, fascinating observant hikers with their beauty and endurance: to think that a tiny pink flower can blossom in such a harsh, unforgiving climate. Depending on the time of year, low growing blueberry bushes beckon with powerfully sweet berries. And it is simply breathtaking in the best sense to stand near the rooftop of eastern North America, knowing firsthand about the physical endurance and psychological strength needed to touch the sky. "Some hard climbing," exclaimed Medusa, "But God! Is it beautiful!"

As the hikers crossed the Whites, many took advantage of the Appalachian Mountain Club huts to make their way through. The huts, filled primarily with short-term hikers, provide dinner, bunk space, water, and breakfast. When they're lucky, thru-hikers can exchange work for food and a bunk in the huts, something that allows them to carry less food in their packs or stretch dwindling food supplies longer, and enjoy a bunk out of the weather. The downside is that hikers, always hungry, must wait until "paying guests" have eaten in order to eat their dinner. Mr. Bean worked at two of the huts, as did Wanderlust. Cygnus Swan worked at Zealand Falls hut, and remembered to thank the croo there. "You put up with us changing music tapes every five minutes, putting flat things in the 'stir things' drawer, scraping every last bit of food on the plates into our mouths and still provided us 'awesome' bunk space!" K-Posa and Sandman worked at both Zealand Falls and then again at Lakes of the Clouds huts. "Since we had worked at Zealand, we already knew the drill. When we got to Lakes, the croo was new. On top of that, they had 96 people there that night, so they were glad to get the help."

As the hikers make their way through the Whites, many come to feel as Walk with Wong did. "This beautiful weather makes me wake up every morning knowing that this new day is going to be my best yet on the Trail." Scout evidently found nirvana while hiking in the Whites. "Everyday and every way, the views are getting better and better. I am so pumped to get up in the morning. Great views all day, only to arrive at a hut at two in the afternoon, eat 'til I burst, hike up and down the river or the falls, take a two-hour nap, enjoy some of what [hiker] Let It Be is known for, and finish the day off with a meteor shower!"

Getting through the Whites means that the hiker has arrived in Maine. Finally. And Maine is where the Holy Mountain is.

But although the hikers have only 275 miles left to walk, just a little over 10 percent of the Trail left, some of the miles are over the roughest terrain the Trail has to offer. "But nobody ever talks about how hard southern Maine is," noted K-Posa. "They'll tell you to get ready for the Whites, to watch for the wind, not to underestimate the conditions above treeline. And they'll lie about how flat Shenandoah is. But nobody ever talks about southern Maine." Marmot agreed with that assessment. "If I had known it was this tough, I might not have started hiking." Probably Wildhair was luckiest as he passed through southern Maine. He hiked along with Just Harry, a hiker who had hiked from Harper's Ferry to Katahdin 10 times. Wildhair benefited from Just Harry's knowledge of the Trail. "From Gorham to Stratton," Just Harry advised Wildhair, "that will be the hardest."

In addition to the rugged peaks, the Trail in southern Maine is dominated by two features: Mahoosuc Notch and Mahoosuc Arm. Together they comprise only three miles or so of the Trail. But what a three miles it is. Ask a hiker about a bear and she'll smile and tell you how close she was to a mother and cub. Ask another hiker about his boots falling apart, and he'll brag about how he limped for days with his feet flopping on the muddy Trail. All of them have trudged through snow and rain, so being wet is no big deal. But ask hikers about the Mahoosuc Notch and watch their eyes turn distant. Every hiker remembers his or her passage through one of Nature's best obstacles courses.

Mahoosuc Notch is routinely called the hardest mile on the Appalachian Trail, and southbounders often try to frighten northbounders about the difficulty. Tom and Millie just took the commentary in stride, saying, "You learn not to listen to anybody till you do it yourself."

What makes Mahoosuc Notch so difficult is that hiking, performed as a lower body exercise, ceases altogether and a free-form, over-under-around-and-through crawl takes its place. Whereas above treeline in the Presidentials hikers can still take steps, in Mahoosuc Notch the hiker must simply stop and look and figure out nearly every step. A hiker must walk, jump, clamber, hoist, crawl, tiptoe, scramble, squeeze, ease, and slide to get through. If the passage through isn't a full-body experience, the hiker obviously wasn't in the Mahoosuc Notch. "It wasn't tough by any stretch of the imagination," reflected Nomad, "but I can imagine it would be sucking if you have to go through it alone or in the pouring rain."

The reason for the rocky crawl is a grand collection of sharp-edged, house-sized boulders that have collected in the Notch. Nomad, Al, Just Pete, and Monkey Butt made it their challenge to go through without removing their packs. "It took a little over an hour and we laughed almost the entire way under sunny blue skies. It was really neat to see the snow and ice tucked away in some of the corners and it was coolly refreshing to feel the chill of it. Only Al and I made it through without taking our packs off. Monkey Butt got caught going through one of the small squeezes and was stuck for a bit. He was like a turtle caught upside down." Passing through the Notch reminded Gutsy "of playing chess, trying to figure out where to go next." Firefly made it through in about two hours, noting that her "legs were so short and the boulders are so big that finding a way to climb was hard." K-Posa made the mistake of resupplying in Gorham and then having to tote his full and heavy pack through the Notch. "I had seven days' worth of food in my pack. I'll never do that again. It's hard hopping from ledge to ledge with a full pack on your back." Hikers must often stop to help their hiking partners, as did Breakin' Wind. Turtle was plugging along with two broken fingers, which made it even more difficult for him to get through. Breakin' Wind helped by giving Turtle a step up here and there. Mr. Honeymooner noted that pranksters were having sport with hikers. "Instead of white blazes, the Notch is marked with arrows that are supposed to help you find your way through. But some jokers have been up there and a lot of the boulders are decorated with white arrows, and so you really have no clue about which way to go."

Then, upon spending anywhere from 50 minutes to three hours coming through Mahoosuc Notch, the hiker must climb up Mahoosuc Arm, another vertical climb up a rock wall. "It nearly killed me," said Greywolf shaking his head. Allgood flirted with injury trying to climb Mahoosuc Arm. "I fell 10 feet down trying to cross the cliffs." "It was simply straight up," recalled Mr. Honeymooner. "I'd gladly go through the Notch again, but I don't ever want to climb up Mahoosuc Arm." Gutsy had a better time with her traverse of the Notch and Arm. She opted to come through the Notch, tent for the night and then pull the Arm the next morning. Lucky for Bloody Nose, he found his second wind in Mahoosuc Notch. As he struggled through the Whites, spending several days sick between Pinkham Notch and Gorham and not knowing if he would be able to shake the crud and fatigue, he finally found redemption. "The day I 'walked' through Mahoosuc Notch was the turning point and I've felt the best I've felt on the whole trip since."

As hikers plod through the last 700 miles of Appalachian Trail, a final metamorphosis takes place. Whether it is positive or negative depends entirely upon the hiker.

Physical changes deepen. Thru-hiking men have a starved, Eastern European look about their faces. It's hard to see on the men who let their beards grow, but on the few who haven't, the sunken, hollow cheeks emphasize what so many of them say: "I never get enough to eat these days." The poor man's Power Bar, a Snickers, doesn't really contribute enough of the kinds of calories hikers need. Their shoulders look small and their collar bones appear to be covered by only the thinnest expanse of skin. Their upper body strength, what's left of it, is hard to see. Their arms don't exactly look shrunken, only small. Abdomens are flat, waists concave. Hikers who started with extra padding around the middle have long since lost it, and it would be difficult, if not impossible, to find a waistline that's more than 34 inches among them. The hikers' legs have a polished and glossy appearance at skin surface, but look stringy and sinewy just the same. It's easy to see blue veins riding across the top of a corded thigh and calf muscles just under the skin. Some hikers talk about how their feet have widened. Interestingly, the most developed muscle seems to be the inside of the front quadriceps, at the knee. This muscle, strong from constant use, looks like an misplaced knob.

Thru-hiking women also have a different appearance. They are not spare and gaunt in the way that the men are. Rather, the women have a tough and solid look. Many miles earlier they lost their body fat and became more muscular. Most have legs that look like they could remodel houses by kicking down walls. The women tend to look more healthy than the men, even if their rugged appearance seems way out of kilter with advertising images of feminine beauty. They exude a confidence that most women don't wear. They know the price they've paid, and they know that the confidence wasn't purchased at the cosmetics counter in the local department store.

Since Georgia, most hikers have tried to keep an open and tolerant attitude about their hike, as well as others'. Trail tolerance is the most highly prized precept of etiquette there is; many hikers come to the Trail to escape the incessant advice that comes from all quarters of modern life—friends, colleagues, media, family—about how to conduct their lives. Hikers may ponder each other's hiking style, like wondering why Bare would want to hike barefooted or why a person would want to have a hiking partner instead of hike alone, but for the most part, they are content to let it go at that—just pondering or casual conversation. But as the accumulating fatigue exacts its price, what was once a joyful attitude of tolerance and "hike your own hike" turns to an attitude of Trail-beaten and weary. Some hikers are as frayed as the binding on their Tevas. For many of the '96 hikers, the changes set in during the 40 miles in Connecticut. There seemed to be an insurmountable wall of bone-tired fatigue for many. Morning Glory, who left Springer with five other partners was now the only one of her group left on the Trail, and even she "thought about leaving," when she crossed Connecticut. Hobbes, of Calvin and Hobbes noted, "It was really a problem. Overuse injuries seemed to be more prevalent as hikers try to put in miles that they shouldn't. Most hikers no longer have any reserves of body fat to rely upon. And lots of them are slowing down. They're tired of walking in the rain, so they don't. They just can't be bothered with that."

Some hikers seemed to lose their sense of humor and as they did so, their critiques of each other increased. Hobbes noted that "we all say 'hike your own hike,' but almost nobody means it anymore. Everyone is checking out everyone else's mileage. Some hikers are really angry at others who have more time and more money to spend on their hikes. And there seems to be an incredible set of rules that thru-hikers use to distinguish between thru-hikers and non-thru-hikers. Sometimes in a shelter other thru-hikers won't talk to us. They'll ignore us because they think we're day hikers, since we carry a change of clothes for the shelter. When they see we're thru-hiking, then they'll talk to us."

In many cases, as Katahdin becomes closer, confidence becomes arrogance for some. Although the hikers came to the sanctuary because they said they were tired of society's arbitrary rules, some hikers start making their own set of arbitrary rules. Several southbounders, with only a couple of hundred miles on their boots and not yet Trail-hardened, crossed paths with northbounders who were nearing Katahdin. The southbounders were quizzed on whether or not they had forded the Kennebec River, as if doing so made a hiker a "real" thru-hiker. The discussions of various hikers' Trail purity—or lack thereof—increased, and a few day-hikers reported receiving the cold shoulder from thru-hikers, once their day-hiking status had been made clear.

Some thru-hikers developed a misguided sense of Trail ownership and began to act as if they and they alone were welcomed to hike the Trail, that others should go elsewhere. Their attitudes have some merit, because for nearly 2,000 miles, thru-hikers have repeatedly seen the trashy and occasionally filthy calling cards of careless and thoughtless people left behind on the Trail and in the parks that the Trail passes through. (KFC boxes, anyone? Mickey D hamburger bags? Cigarette butts: that's always a nice addition to the landscape, isn't it?) It would be hard to know where the trash was worst. The Smokies? Pine Grove Furnace? Bear Mountain? As overused and overburdened as the Appalachian Trail may be—"You can't swing a dead cat by the tail without hitting someone out here," said Buc-Buc about the crowds of people coming out to enjoy the quiet of a wilderness experience—it was Benton MacKaye's vision that a trail be built so that all people might have an escape from the plagues of industrialism. That the Trail is so popular only underscores and justifies MacKaye's original vision. It's hard to fault thru-hikers for wanting to protect a trail that has given them so much.

Other thru-hikers noted with regret that their fellow hikers started taking Trail Angels and Trail Magic for granted. "In the beginning of a thru-hike, hikers think that Trail Magic is a wonderful experience. Later, if there aren't enough Cokes left in the cooler to go around, hikers may leave a nasty-gram in the register," Hobbes observed. Lazy Bones, a repeat hiker, seconded the observation, saying, "There didn't used to be as many Trail Angels out here, and now to some extent the experience is handed out to the hikers. Worse than that, some hikers seem to abuse the good works, like hitchhiking in for the Thursday night dinner at the Church of the Mountain, then timing their hike to be there on the next Thursday night, and then hitchhiking back for yet a third time. Some stay three or four nights without bothering about a donation. Some hikers are just trying to take advantage of someone trying to do them a favor." Lazy Bones was not alone in noticing the abuse; other hikers expressed regret that Trail Angels were abused in this way.

Other hikers start thinking that the Trail Magic happened to them *because* they are hikers, not because Trail Angels happen to be generous people. As Wanderlust and other hikers pointed out, "until you've gone on other adventures, you might think that the Appalachian Trail is the only place where people exhibit this kind of generous behavior. The fact is, you can find it anywhere if you take the time to look."

Occasionally hikers become rude to onlookers who are interested enough to inquire into the endeavor; they've answered the same questions so many times before. For nearly all of the hikers, answering the standard questions—"How much does your pack weigh?" "How do you eat?" "Did you really walk all of the way here?"—was fun in the beginning. Their eyes would light up and their faces would smile as they described how far they had walked and what the hike was like. But as confidence turns to arrogance or fatigue breeds impatience, some hikers take on a look of bored condescension as they answer the questions again. On occasion it is obvious that unless the inquisitors look as if they might offer a handout, the thru-hikers cluster into their own group, oblivious to others around them, transmitting loud and clear the belief that others "can't possibly understand." Some routinely belittle the fact that other people visit a mountain summit by way of asphalt and a car, forgetting that at some point in their pasts and probably again one day in their futures, driving to a mountaintop may be all that they can manage, too.

For the majority of hikers, however, their final transformation on the way to Katahdin inspires. These hikers have discovered that the views they've enjoyed from the mountain summits have led them to a view far superior to any offered upon a mountaintop: the view inside themselves where they have wrestled with personal weaknesses, discovered strength, found endurance, laughter, joy, and peace. This view they have of themselves and of what's important in the world reveals how trivial much of what contemporary life serves up as the daily, standard ration.

Instead of becoming haughty with this newfound knowledge, these hikers are both humbled by it and revel in it. Men and women, regardless of their physical appearance, wear an intriguing, remote look upon their faces. The well of internal motivation that they have relied upon for so long comes to the surface. They know that they have changed and they are grateful. And it is this feeling that draws the community of thru-hikers, both current and past, together.

Some hikers find that their experiences along the Trail validate what they have suspected all along: that there is something assuring about the quiet of a day spent alone, something wondrous in watching other wildlife go about its day, something beautiful in soaking in a sunset or sunrise and being a part of the world as it spins in daily revolution. They realize that prior to their hikes they had been too separated from the natural world and that a close and intimate connection with the natural world is far more important than the conveniences and contrivances that modern life has to offer. They are no longer the willing and easy prey of a world where commercial interests routinely look for ways to concoct and exploit personal fears. Moreover, they are no longer willing to be distracted by the contemporary noise. They would rather be comforted by the music of wind in the trees and songbirds.

Some hikers are lucky enough to find the words to describe these changes. Glider explained it saying, "Being out in the mountains every day is the best part. For me, hiking in the mountains has always been this intensely spiritual experience. The hiking works your body into shape, while the scenery works on your spirit. I doubt that there's any better recipe for overall health." Bandana Light realized it, saying, "After the physical part and the joy of pure escapism passes, it becomes a journey of the soul. A journey to my true self, which had taken a few detours the last few years." H could also wrap words around the experience. "That is why all the Trail Angels bless us for doing what seems such a selfish thing. They see the pure unaffected life shining from our eyes . . . and we're all out here swearing, swankering, running naked, telling jokes, farting, philosophizing, communicating intensely . . . we dedicate entire days to humor, love, food, sleep, sun, rain, full moons, streams, and views . . . we are at our richest, our most alive. That's why some days can be so painful, too. It's life in the raw!"

Other hikers who try to talk about these changes are often at a loss to describe them. They are like Louis Armstrong who, when asked to describe rhythm, said, that rhythm is "what if you've got it, you don't need a definition; and if you don't got it, no definition is any good." Words fail them, and hiker after hiker will shake his or her head, cast a look down to the ground, pause a moment, raise their eyes again and say, "I can't describe it. I just can't describe it." But they know that whatever It may be, that It is real. And they know, too, that they can never fully return to the way they used to lead their lives and the way they used to see the world, whatever that might have been. Many of them begin to dread the end of their hikes because they're just not sure how they will integrate this new knowledge into their lives. Too much that matters has changed. The frenetic, and occasionally pointless, pace of life back home no longer holds any charms.

The mystical experience the hikers struggle to explain was once described by William James, who noted that the mystical experience has several facets: It defies expression; it provides an overwhelming sense of understanding, in that a person sees the unity of the universe and his own integration in it; it causes the person to see the universe not as a dead machine, but as a living presence; it reminds a person that the universe of which he is a part is overwhelming; it is brief, but from one recurrence to another it is susceptible to continuous development; that what is felt as inner richness is important; that it forces passivity on the person as the person feels that another power takes over.

People who experience a mystical interlude often talk about the deep and profound peace that they find, the sense of joy and laughter, a loss of concern about worldly problems, and the heightened emotional intensity that they feel. The word that best describes this experience, though terribly cheapened by today's coarsened language, is *ecstasy*. If ecstasy is "a state of exalted delight in which normal understanding is felt to be surpassed," then surely *this* is what many, many thru-hikers have come to understand on their way to Katahdin.

s e p t e m b e r

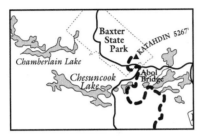

ALL GOOD THINGS COME IN ALL GOOD TIME.

I'M THROUGH HIKING.

-Allgood

In late August and September, the world goes back to work, thankful for that brief respite from a clock-governed life called "vacation." What they go back to, they inevitably find, has changed very little: the same-old same-old prevails.

When, in late August and September, the White Mountains of New Hampshire are behind a hiker and not ahead, when the Mahoosuc Notch is finally behind a hiker and not ahead, when the twenty 3,000-plus feet peaks of southern Maine are finally behind and not ahead, then the Trail experiences that have opened doors to new perspectives on life and living build to a Hallelujah Chorus that only Handel can compete with. When the Bigelow range is behind—"I guess that's the last big climb before the end . . . sad in a way, but my knees are happy," observed Nomad—a thru-hiker becomes a bona fide 2,000 miler. Immediately the hikers set their sights on the last four major parts of the Trail: the Kennebec River, the town of Monson, the 100 Mile Wilderness, and the ascent of the Holy Mountain itself.

The northbound hikers who cross into Maine often find a special kind of northwoods magic, a point of pride with the Maine Appalachian Trail Club. They work hard to protect Maine's reputation of "forever wild." Difficult and rugged though the Trail may be, in Maine the

Appalachian Trail can be achingly beautiful. This, compounded by the joy—and relief—that many of the hikers begin to feel as they near Katahdin, makes hiking in Maine possibly the best part of the entire trip.

By day, mosses and ferns carpet the Trail and big, round boulders punctuate it. Streams and brooks with lapis blue water chuckle by. The world is a collage of blue and green as spruce and fir and hemlock perfume the air. Maples dance red flames next to the white bark of birch trees. By twilight, ponds, too many to count, glisten like rosy mirrors in the glow of a northwoods sunset. Evergreen trees frame the land with deep blue spires. Clouds that by day were white, puffy cotton balls become at night deep purple pillows. Ungainly but nonetheless romantic, moose amble by, adding a touch of wonder. Too bad there was no Appalachian Trail for Albert Bierstadt to paint. He might have preferred it to the Rockies. "Maine," remarked Wildhair, "had everything."

But that's when the weather is fine and the skies are clear. When it rains in Maine—and in 1996 some said it rained everyday—hiking is a dismal affair. In September 1846, Henry David Thoreau set out to explore what he called the "backwoods of Maine." He intended to go during the "driest part of a dry season," September. Yet as he approached Katahdin from Bangor, he noted that "the primitive wood is always and everywhere damp and mossy," and that he "traveled constantly with the impression that [he] was in a swamp." Thoreau doesn't mention whether New England had experienced a wet spring or three hurricanes as did the Class of '96. It would be interesting to welcome Thoreau back for a ghostly chat with the Class of '96 so that they could compare hiking stories. Many thru-hikers would probably have only one question: "Did you have to ford a stream or two, or three, Mr. Henry David, or the entire state, like we did?"

The Maine Appalachian Trail Club (MATC) calls the Kennebec River the "most formidable unbridged crossing along the entire 2,100 mile AT." This is the normal warning posted under normal circumstances. Trail conditions in 1996, however, were far from normal. If raging streams and brooks normally unmarked on the maps were giving hikers problems, what would the Kennebec be like?

Although the ford looks easy enough—there is no steep gorge like the Nantahala River and there certainly isn't the width of the Potomac River—the MATC and Appalachian Trail Conference operate a free ferry for the hikers. Approximately 70 yards wide, the Kennebec resembles a western river with its expansive, swift, and powerful current. Watching the ferryman paddle hikers across reveals just how strong the river is. Upon picking up a hiker on the southern bank, the ferryman must paddle upstream against the current for 50 yards. It's tough and slow work, but must be done so that the ferryman has a decent shot of hitting the take-out on the northern side of the river. Then, paddling on a diagonal, the ferryman crosses to mid-river, and then lets the current push the canoe downstream to the northern bank while the ferryman serves as the rudder. Even with the river doing the work past mid-stream, the ferryman and hiker are often still breathing hard when they arrive on the northern side of the Kennebec.

Hikers are warned as early as New Hampshire that fording the Kennebec is dangerous. An upstream dam can and does release water faster than a hiker can cross. Plus the yearly four-to-five feet thick accumulation of glacial ice along the river banks each year changes the river bottom and therefore the dynamics of the water. Steve Longley, the ferryman, sees his charge to get hikers safely across the river as an international responsibility. Hikers come from across the world to hike the Appalachian Trail and sooner or later for the hikers, the Trail stops at the Kennebec. In 1996, the Kennebec was merciless; backed up water from hurricanes Bertha, Edouard, and Hortense saw to that. Water releases were more frequent and when they took place, more prolonged.

Whether or not a hiker should attempt to ford the Kennebec elicits strong emotions and comments from hikers as well as the ferrymen. Some hikers argue that the Kennebec is a "wilderness river" and as such should be forded since it crosses a "wilderness trail." If one doesn't ford the wilderness river then somehow one has not had a complete "wilderness experience." Other hikers noted that they've crossed other rivers along the Appalachian Trail without having to ford them—the French Broad, the Shenandoah, the Potomac, the Susquehanna, the Delaware, the Hudson, the Housatonic, to name a few—so why should they put their life on the line for the Kennebec? Barry, a '93 thru-hiker and assistant ferryman, said that he'd consider painting a white blaze on the bow of his canoe, if it would help the purists feel better about paddling across instead of fording.

Some hikers see the Kennebec as just one more problem to solve, and since they have become accustomed to solving their problems, they try to ford the river. Some hikers, such as Mucho Gusto, came across OK. Others did too, but not without a good dose of fear.

Barry the Ferryman helping Quid Pro Quo cross the Kennebec.

Nomad, Monkey Butt, and Al decided to ford the river. "It was Monkey Butt's wish," said Nomad "so Al and I went with him. We got there early in the morning and had to bushwhack through chest-high grass to get to the gravel bars where it is easier crossing. Off came the boots, on went the sandals, and away we went. We did pack everything into plastic bags, not that it would have helped because you'd probably have to ditch your pack if you got swept away.

"The first two sections went fairly well. The water was about thigh high, and it got the adrenaline going. I was a bit concerned about it as the water was fairly strong and forceful. I was the last of the three going across, though we were only about 20 feet or so apart. The third section was a whole different story. The water is deeper and runs faster, and this is where the problems started.

"Monkey Butt went first—he's a serious kayaker, so he could read the water a bit—and was quickly up to his midriff in water. He had to turn back to the second gravel bar. Al and I started to follow him a little upstream, and when he headed back, so did we. There was a southbounder on the far shore who arrived and was watching us. He pointed out that downstream about 20 feet it was more shallow and that crossing would be easier.

"Monkey Butt and Al were off slowly, but I was pretty worried at this point. I wasn't even sure I'd make it back over the other two sections if I had to. I was pretty pooped and all the adrenaline in my body was making me shake. I started in after them, though a bit upstream from them still.

"I was amazed by the force of the water. I had a hard time even standing in one spot. By this time, the other two were done and were taking their packs off. I had frozen and couldn't move, forwards or backwards, and was close to panicking.

"The water started slowly to rise. By now it had reached my belly button and was sometimes lapping up to my chest. Al and MB kept telling me to back up (go downstream) to where they had crossed: it was shallower there. But I just couldn't get myself to lift my feet and do anything. I felt that if I budged at all, I'd be swept away, and I remember how vividly my hiking poles held me up but vibrated from the force of the water. I could hear them.

"So the two of them jumped back into the water and waded out to me. They walked upstream from me to break the force of the water a bit and to give me moral support. It was easier going after that, and I made it across.

"I was shaking like a leaf when I got to the other side. We were pretty wiped out once we were done, and spent a fair amount of time in Caratunk at the store relaxing, eating, and drying out."

Scout, who crossed with Mucho Gusto, wasn't as lucky as her partner. "Sitting on the beach [at Pleasant Pond] trying to get collected again after scaring the hell out of myself. Fell in three times, where Mucho, eddying behind me, somehow caught me and put me back on my feet before I was swept downstream by the current." 007 also gave the ford a fair try, but couldn't. "The Kennebec River was not to be. I tried to swim it, but turned back to take the canoe." The majority of hikers who had been lucky enough to reach the Kennebec saw no reason to jeopardize their hike. Like Gutsy, in the "spirit of self-propelled locomotion," they would take the canoe and help paddle.

Some hikers, however, wanted to make the ford the ultimate test of manliness. Chuck of the Buns of Steel Gang, remarked to "all you guys who used the ferry: this shows your testosterone levels have gotten too low and may be tilting toward the feminine side." AT Actioneer, a hiking partner, simply ribbed Chuck, saying, "Before Chuck attempted his ford, he was shaking and weeping uncontrollably. He kept repeating, 'Hold me, just hold me.' So I gave him a hug and told him he wouldn't be any less of a man if he took the boat and kept his boots dry."

After the drenching that Hurricane Hortense gave the state—depending on a hiker's whereabouts he or she saw anywhere from four to seven inches of rain in mid-September—fording the Kennebec became that much more dangerous. Hungry Hiker was lucky to be alive. As Firefly told the story, "he started out OK, even looked good, but then the water started to rise. While just starting into the third and deepest channel, the water started to rush, covering the gravel bars quickly and leaving him stranded . . . he was trapped . . . Steve the Wonder Canoeist paddled after him." Steve was nearly pitched in the river himself, when Hungry Hiker attempted to get in the canoe, pack and all, on the first hoist. The extra weight nearly flipped the canoe. Finally, though, Hungry Hiker got safely into the canoe and was ferried to the northern shore. "In retropsect," said Hungry Hiker, "it was a stupid decision to cross the river on foot . . . I sat on the shoreline for 45 minutes thinking 'should I?' or 'shouldn't I?' It looked benign and it lulled me to sleep."

As an added bonus for the 1996 thru-hikers, the Kennebec wasn't the only dangerous river crossing. Other rivers raged through the Maine woods, and hikers were either lucky or unlucky depending on when they arrived. Rivers that would normally pose no problem claimed a hiker here or there, as did smaller brooks and streams that were swollen. Hikers happened upon many unmarked streams that, were it a typical year, wouldn't have been there at all. When there was a Trail, it was a sloppy, soupy affair. Sometimes simply getting to the Kennebec proved to be difficult. Acutely aware of the ferryman's hours, Cough Drop ran down the Trail making sure to reach the Kennebec in time. Did he make it? "Oh yeah," he replied, "but I left a face print in the mud in the middle of the Trail."

Because of the extraordinarily wet year, hikers joked about renaming the Appalachian Trail the Appalachian Flume and many arrived in Monson ready to rename the Trail town "Monsoon." It would have been appropriate: Hurricane Bertha had made life miserable for early season hikers, Hurricane Edouard dallied with the mid-season bunch, and Hurricane Hortense finished the job by turning on the spigot full-tilt boogie on the late-season hikers. Everywhere the Trail was under water, again. What had been a dam at Pierce Pond Lean-to became a major waterfall. Morning Glory, arriving in Monson with Julie McCoy, Cruise Director, simply shook her head and said that she "should have bought this T-shirt in Norwich: 'I swam the AT in 1996.'" Ajax, who made it across the Kennebec the day before Hortense arrived noted that he "was swept away by the raging torrent that was the Trail—only 5.7 miles today, but I'm in here for good. I could make a lot of jokes about the rain, but it's just not all that funny." Sven, hiking up from the Kennebec to Pleasant Pond Lean-to a few days later, had to bushwhack for two miles because the heavy rain had created uncharted brooks and turned the Trail into a mini-waterfall.

Keith and Pat Shaw, proprietors of the rambling, white-frame Shaw's Boarding House, did everything in their power to help hikers rise above the dismal Trail conditions. With Keith and Pat in charge, how could hikers not feel better about their hike?

Shaw's holds a special place in the hearts (and certainly the stomachs) of over 20,000 hikers. To southbounders, Shaw's serves the same purpose that the Walasi-Yi Center in Neels Gap does for northbounders: It's the first place after starting a thru-hike where a hiker can come in, take a shower, sleep in a bed, get a meal, and collect themselves. To section hikers, hanging out at Shaw's provides a way to vicariously have the thru-hiking experience. To northbounders, it is the last place to enjoy before entering the remote 100 Mile Wilderness. The emphasis is on *enjoy* and, not surprisingly, to hikers who have walked over 2,000 miles, *enjoy* means *food*. And to be sure, Shaw's does not disappoint. Keith's breakfasts are the stuff legends are made of.

"How do you want your eggs? . . . They're jumbo eggs . . . Brown jumbo eggs . . . You want cheese in them? . . . Pancakes? . . . I got blueberry pancakes . . . How many you want? . . . How many bacon? . . . You want sausage? . . . How many? . . . You want toast with that? . . . I got toast . . . You like hash browns? . . . How about some hash browns?" When the made-to-order breakfast, a huge mountain of food, is ready, Keith, his blue eyes twinkling, puts it in front of hikers and casually asks "How's that look to you?" As if he doesn't know it's a work of art.

The soft-spoken Pat takes care of the evening meal, cooking nearly all day to put an equally hearty spread before the hikers. If hikers haven't developed a boarding house reach by the time they reach Shaw's, they will before they leave. Keith and Pat will see to it. ("Sure you don't want some more eggs? . . . I have some more pancakes over here . . . Any more toast? . . . Is that all you're going to eat? . . . How 'bout you? . . . You get enough? . . . Everybody here get enough? . . . Here, eat this . . . There's still food on the table.") Keith will certainly see to it that northbound hikers tank up before they leave Monson. If they don't, they have no one to blame but themselves.

But hikers know sincerity when they see it and they respond to Keith and Pat's hospitality. Crazy Toes "made it to the infamous Shaw's" and recognized that "It's worth every step I've taken since Georgia!" Paco testified to Keith's salesmanship, noting that "Had I eaten much more, I may have exploded." Bloody Nose enjoyed two days with Keith, noting that "Boy, this is just what I needed before I head into the final week on this wonderful journey." Plus the hikers were grateful for the help Keith rendered in other ways: After sloshing about for days on the soggy Trail, Greyhound appreciated Keith turning on the furnace in his barn to help her dry her boots. Spare was thankful for the early morning jump-start out the door Keith provided. And for sure Keith spent his summer, between flipping pancakes and urging hikers to eat, answering questions about Big Wilson Stream.

Although Shaw's brings a smile to thru-hiker faces, it also puts a lump in their throats. Hiker emotions run rampant as reality sets in: only 116 miles or so before their journey is over. So close to Katahdin, Shaw's dining tables become a stage where hikers relive the adventures and challenges of the last several months.

Many hikers talk about the psychological challenges of hiking the Appalachian Trail. "Like walking in the rain," noted Mr. Honeymooner. "You gotta walk in the rain. I can't tell you how many times I fell. I lost count a long time ago. And you know you have only yourself to blame. It's not like anybody nudged you. You can't look up and blame somebody else. You know you put your foot down wrong. So you just have to pick yourself up and keep going if you intend to get there."

The tables are also where hikers feel the pull of Katahdin pulsing in their veins. Sir Goober Peas felt it. "Weather permitting, we will have fun upon the Big Mountain. I haven't seen it yet, but I can start to smell it." Cygnus Swan, who left Springer Mountain with embers burning in her stomach, felt those embers burning again. "Giddy, drunk on Keith's breakfasts, I breathe deep and prepare for the final miles—despite the gorging I've a pit in my stomach and an excitement." Lazy Bones, nearing his goal of a second thru-hike, noted that as "I finish this splendid adventure, my thoughts will include all of the Trail community who provide so much to the hiking community." Wistfulness and relief pervaded Cosmo's thoughts. "Feeling a mixture of elation and sadness . . . after this no more mail drops, no more shopping, no more washing the gear, in short: the lifestyle I've come to love is almost *kaput*! Seven more nights in the woods and then I'm in a car, rolling down an asphalt ribbon unraveling a 1000 miles south to a new life, a new job, new possibilities, new *unknowns*. I'll miss this Trail, but *damn, I'm tired*!" Firefly was ready to move on to other things. "I'm sad but I want to get this over with.

Maybe if the weather had been nicer, I'd feel differently." Shaft regretted that upon leaving Shaw's he was leaving the Trail altogether. "Well, this is good-bye. My juggling act of finance just came crashing down . . . it got me far, farther than most, but short of the mark many of you shall hit. The frustration is multi-faceted . . . hindsight is 20/20 . . . all the gas, restaurants and beer could have fueled my hike another 400 miles." Gumby, who celebrated his birthday at Shaw's, felt a keen balance. "Sad to end the only life I've known for six months, but happy to get on with the next chapter, whatever it will be."

As hikers prepare to leave Monson, their eyes have that remote look, as if somewhere deep beneath the surface they are conducting an internal conversation. Their gear is clean, their stomachs are full, their faces may be smiling. They've picked up their final food drop. But the conversation they are having cannot be heard. As the hikers put on their socks and boots and prepare for the final miles, it is obvious what that conversation is about. It is an unspoken conversation between the hiker and his feet and the last remaining miles to be covered.

Most people just put their shoes on with little thought. Just slide the feet in or tighten the laces and go. It's something that they do as easily as breathing. Even day hikers tend to put on their boots with little or no thought. But a well-seasoned, Trail-hardened hiker dons his or her boots with private ceremony.

Sitting in a chair or on a bench, a hiker will first gently cradle the foot at the ankle, taking care to brush aside anyway grit or dirt, maybe even treating the foot to a massage. The hiker does this almost absent-mindedly. Then the hiker will flex and point the foot, work the arch and maybe wiggle the toes. Then there's the absent-minded check for grit between the toes and a finger check of toenails, if any should be left. Before relegating the foot to the confinement of a sock, the darkness of a boot, and the weight of a full pack, the hiker will make sure that the foot has a fighting chance at comfort.

Then the hiker checks the boot. Is the boot tongue pulled forward enough to make a comfortable opening? Are the laces loose enough to accommodate the entry of a foot? If the boot passes muster, the hiker will then tap the boot to make sure no small pebbles or twigs lie upon the sole. If something drops from the boot toe, the hiker will tap the boot again to

Caspar's trail-weary boots.

be sure that all obstructions fall out. If nothing falls, the hiker checks the laces and tongue once again before putting on the boot. He engages in a few ankle circles to loosen the joint, and then steps into the boot.

Then the hiker methodically tightens the laces. Depending upon the particular foot problems of each hiker, the laces may skip the first set of eyelets. In any event, the hiker doesn't just tighten the top criss-cross of a boot lace. The hiker carefully tightens each criss-cross working the foot up and down at the shoe break, making sure that the boot is ready for uphill pushes as well as downhill breaking. It's been a long five or six months and now is no time to inflict more than the customary ration of foot pain. Finally the first foot is securely in the boot. The hiker turns attention to the other foot and the ceremony begins again. A foot must be prepared for the final stretch.

Between Monson and Katahdin lies the 100 Mile Wilderness. Although not truly a wilderness due to the number of dirt logging roads that cut across the terrain, this portion of the Trail is remote and cannot and should not be underestimated. The land is generally used for hunting and is crossed only by deeply rutted, occasionally unmaintained, rocky, logging roads. There are no towns "nearby." There isn't much traffic on the paved roads to make hitching a ride easy, and even the major paved roads go for miles without power lines, a true oddity in today's electrified world. And just because a hiker reaches Monson successfully doesn't guarantee that he or she will still be able to reach Katahdin. There may be only 116 miles left—roughly five hundredths of the distance of the Trail—but anything can happen. The words of Wingfoot come back to haunt: "No, good luck to you. You'll need it."

Allgood was indeed lucky: five miles just before Monson, he woke up feverish and nauseated and wondered if he were going to die. It would have been preferable. The pain and nausea were unlike anything he'd ever experienced before. By Monson he'd passed a kidney stone. A local doctor questioned his ability to continue, but Allgood felt he could. He had come too far not to try. Had the timing of the attack been any later, Allgood would probably have been evacuated from the Wilderness, and unable to finish his hike.

Some of what happened in the 100 Mile Wilderness was good fortune made manifest. After hiking together since February, Raindrop and Hibird became engaged on top of Saddleback Mountain. K-Posa had to ford the West Branch of the Pleasant River three times: once to take Nu-Tek the dog across, once to go back and get his pack, and then a third time to come across with his pack. Fortunately for K-Posa, his luck held out. And for starving hikers, there's a potential smorgasbord to be had at each shelter: As hikers draw closer to Katahdin and realize that they're going to make it with food left over, they lighten their pack weight by leaving behind all manners of things for other hikers to eat.

Other hikers were not so lucky. Hiker after hiker had trouble with the raging water of Big Wilson Stream. Sir Goober Peas and Aunt Jemima made it across, but just barely, enough to make Sir Goober Peas wonder if he were going to die right there at the AT. The stream felled Six Pack, and a few days later, Will-Make-It. The falls were painful enough, but because of the cold water, Will-Make-It nearly fell victim to hypothermia. Tom and Millie went through the Wilderness in four days because the steady downpour made the hiking so dismal. "I hiked 23 miles just to get to Daicey Pond and nearly got hypothermia in the downpour that I later learned was Hortense."

Mrs. Honeymooner, after slackpacking Mr. Honeymooner and others up the Trail, wanted to hike the Wilderness with her husband and finish on Katahdin with him. It was to be the perfect end to a unique honeymoon. But she sprained her ankle severely some seven miles into the Wilderness.

After hiking all of that distance, Georgia to Maine, Mr. Honeymooner stopped short of completing his hike. It was their honeymoon, and he wasn't going to Katahdin unless his bride could go with him.

What happened to Poly + Ester was heartbreaking. After leaving so many comical notes in registers, giving pep talks to the hikers behind them and endearing themselves to nearly everybody on the Trail, Poly + Ester were unable to finish their hike together. While engaged in conversation with another hiker on the Trail, Ester lost her balance and sustained a compound fracture of her arm on Chairback Mountain. Getting Ester to a road was a tremendous ordeal, and even after they were lucky enough to find a ride, the driver either wouldn't or couldn't take Ester on to find a doctor or hospital. They simply deposited her, broken arm and all, at a pay phone. Poly would have to hike Katahdin with the spirit of Ester, "tag-team style."

Some of what happened in the 100 Mile Wilderness, however, proved to be some of the best comedy of the season. Cygnus Swan was on the White Cap range and was so exhausted by the first hill that she "needed a 'pick me up.' So I decided to hike nude to White Cap Peak. Naked, I'm backpacking along and as I climb to the Cap's peak, I meet an elderly fellow, his wife, and their 20-something grandson. I smile and walk by as they laugh in embarrassed amusement."

"Then I shouted back to them, 'Can you see Katahdin from the top?!'"

"The old Mainer, pipe in mouth replied, 'I can sure see it from heyah!'"

Even in the fresh, early morning light of a clear day, Katahdin glows a deep and burnished iron red as the granite boulders upon the mountain both absorb and reflect the bright orange sunlight of dawn. This mountain clearly stands apart from its contemporaries.

For months Katahdin has existed as an intuitive goal in the minds of the thru-hikers. Slowly along the Trail, however, the mountain becomes a sensory experience. At first hikers feel its magnetic pull. Then they smell it. Upon emerging from the 100 Mile Wilderness at Abol Bridge they can finally see Katahdin as it dominates the Maine landscape.

From a distance, this mountain looks like something thrust up from deep inside the Earth, as if something secret were forced upward into the light and air at great expense to the surface. The rocky crust forms

Mt. Katahdin from Daicey Pond.

rivulets into the trees in a profound and silent handshake between external greenery and internal strength. It is a massive sight, both beautiful and difficult to behold. Although it is not capped by year-round snow like the pretty Mt. Rainier and it doesn't hulk above its peers like the table-topped Long's Peak, Katahdin commands the surrounding landscape for miles. To the Indians the mountain was known as Kette-Adene, the greatest mountain. No person, hiker or otherwise, can help but be awed.

The small camp store at Abol Bridge would, under different circumstances, be an unlikely place for a celebration. There's not much there, really, except a little bit of fishing tackle, a little bit of hunting gear, a few bandanas, and a good assortment of junk food. But in the eyes of the thru-hikers, it might as well be the gates of Heaven. There are Doritos to be bought, Cokes to be guzzled, hot showers to take and a front row seat of Katahdin to enjoy. As family and friends arrive, they back their cars and pickups into spaces so that they can watch for their loved ones to emerge from the woods. For some families, the meeting at Abol Bridge is the first time they've seen their hiker since leaving him or her at Springer Mountain. "I hear he's got an earring," shouted a father waiting for his son to emerge. "I think his Mom will have something to say about that."

Hikers who have already arrived sit in the several plastic chairs at the camp store and talk about how far they've come and what they've endured. Caspar talked about how his feet had grown half a size. Greywolf laughed about his aches and pains. "I remember when I was in Damascus, talking to Damascus Dave, I told him 'I sure hope it begins to come together for me real soon. I'm getting tired of hurting.' I remember him saying 'For some people it never comes together. Some people hurt all of the way, everyday they're out there.' It was just about that time that the Unabomber had been caught and I happened to see him on TV. His hair was messy, he had a beard, and they said he lived out in the woods with no electricity. I looked at myself in the mirror, thought about how I'd been living and laughed to myself, 'He looks like a thru-hiker.' All the Unabomber really needed was a white blaze!" And because he hadn't yet eaten a mac-n-cheese dinner on the trail, Greywolf decided that in order to celebrate his achievement, he'd eat a mac-n-cheese dinner at Daicey Pond Lean-to. If the Amicalola Ranger Station is all nerves and tension, the Abol Bridge camp store is complete relaxation and confidence.

As hikers draw nearer to the end, their emotions again run rampant. Wildhair reflected that "it's funny how your dogs still bark after all those miles." Acorn, pondering his ascent of Katahdin, remembered that "each day I was challenged and knocked down and struggled, but each morning I woke up and was able to go on. I got to [Hurd Brook Shelter] today by promising myself one thing: 'I will not quit.'"

None of them started their hikes intending to grow attached to strangers, yet here they are now, friends for life. What they've been through together is unlike any other experience American life offers. No one twisted an arm to make the hiker go in the first place, and when the hiking was miserable, nothing except personal pride made them stay. Chances are that someone back at home would have been perfectly happy if the hiker did return home, so that life could 'get back to normal.' But through it all—being so smelly that even the bugs wouldn't bite, being covered with daily layers of mud, wishing the feet were a little less grimy, eating the nth meal of mac and cheese—the hikers stayed on the Trail because of the support their fellow hikers gave them. "When I started on March 2nd," wrote Monkey Butt, "I honestly thought I wouldn't see many people. I thought I was ahead. I thought I'd be alone for a while. But I think I'm very glad the rest of you started then too. Because I realize that I needed all of you to be there."

K-Posa, Kiwi, and Trooper at the Abol Bridge camp store, Maine.

None of the hikers started a hike in order to be a hero, yet over the course of five or six months that's exactly what happened. In the eyes of their fellow hikers, each hiker is a hero, whether it's for a wiseacre remark that vanquished the blues, for sharing some morsel to eat, for making room in a shelter, or for cursing the bugs together. Sweet Pea cherished the friendship of her fellow hikers, "It's hard to believe that tomorrow is the day. I know that it will take some time for me to really internalize all that I learned while on this hike, but I do know that without my friends I never, ever, would have had the endurance to make it."

None of them went in search of an education, but the very act of walking 2,000-plus miles forced one upon them. "It's the people you meet that make this journey special," said Blueberry. "It will take me years to distill all the lessons I've learned in these past months," reflected Entropy. "I've walked from winter through spring into summer. I've seen the snow melt and the gray skies clear to reveal trillium and dogwood blossoms and lady slipper. I saw rhododendron, then laurel, then azalea. As I moved north I saw the coniferous forest creep slowly from the highest summits to the lowest valleys. The first towns I visited the people said 'y'all.' Now they say 'you.' And as I sit here, as fall begins to color the leaves of the maples, I realize how much I've seen the world change around me and how much I've changed within. To all whom I've shared this experience with and who have shared theirs with me THANK YOU."

Some of them went in search of self and learned many of the lessons Beater Bomb (quoting from *Chicken Soup for the Soul*) learned:

*After a while you learn the subtle difference between holding a
hand and chaining a soul.*
*And you learn that love doesn't mean leaning and company doesn't
mean security.*
*And you begin to learn that kisses aren't contracts and presents
aren't promises.*
*And you begin to accept your defeats with your head up and your
eyes open, with the grace of an adult not the grief of a child.*
*And you learn to build all your roads today because tomorrow's
ground is too unclear for plans.*
*After a while you learn that even sunshine burns if you get too
much.*
*So plant your own garden and decorate your own soul instead of
waiting for someone to bring you flowers.*
And learn that you really can endure,
That you really are strong,
And you really do have worth.

Other hikers realize the price that people pay with their lives enslaved by payments, their bodies stymied by desk jobs, and their spirits separated from Nature. Realizing this, they vow never to go back to that way of life. Gumby realized it and left in a Trail register as a parting shot a quote from Edward Abbey:

*Don't burn yourselves out. Be as I am, a reluctant enthusiast
and part time crusader. A half-hearted fanatic. Save the other half
of yourself for pleasure and adventure. It is not enough to fight for
the West. It is even more important to enjoy it. While you can. While
it's still out here. So get out there, hunt, fish, mess with your friends,
ramble out yonder, and explore the forests, encounter the griz, climb
a mountain, bag the peaks, run the rivers, breath deep that sweet
and elusive air. Enjoy yourselves. Keep your brain connected to the
body, the body active and alive. And I promise you this one sweet
victory over our enemies, over those deskbound people with their
hearts in safe deposit boxes and their eyes hypnotized by their desk
calendars. I promise you this: you will outlive the bastards.*

As they prepare themselves to hike the last 15 miles, the previous 2,143 pass in review. All of the views, the people, the Magic, all of it. "I remember a glowing sunset on Springer in the freezing cold," said Cygnus Swan ". . . then I remember the newness and excitement . . . my first pint of B+J's . . . and more cold . . . and laughter . . . close friends . . . nude hikes . . . life comes together and stays together when I put one foot before the other." For Bloody Nose, the memories formed a cavalcade of hikers. "I feel incredibly fortunate to have hiked this Appalachian Trail. I've met so many wonderful and positive people (thru-hikers, section hikers, day hikers, non-hikers, dogs, etc.) and experienced many wonders of nature. The memories will last forever." 007 shared the feeling. "I'll pack out more than trash when I leave." The Catskill Eagle recognized it as a love affair that hiking the Appalachian Trail becomes. "Well, I've got to admit this long strange journey is going to be hard to beat. Now I've got to find something else to struggle with, curse at, and ultimately fall in love with. Maybe I'll get married."

As the hikers arrive at Baxter State park, they stage for their final climb either at Daicey Pond Lean-to or Katahdin Stream Campground. Pilgrim, thinking about the imminent climb, remarked, "Tomorrow we climb one last time. I think of friends met and miles past. It's been so hard yet so sweet, locked safely in memory to last . . . may God be blessed for all this . . . Summer's over."

When morning rolls around—for those who can wait until morning; many can't—they climb together in the groups they arrived with. Depending on conditions, many hikers leave in velvet blackness of pre-dawn hours so as to be on this mighty peak at sunrise. It suits their purposes to "dance in the moonlight with the world at their feet," as Sir Goober Peas described it.

Swarms of people arrive every year to attempt the climb, and park rangers at Baxter State Park average at least one rescue a week, sometimes three or four. When Thoreau attempted his ascent of Katahdin, he decided that "the tops of mountains are among the unfinished parts of the globe . . . only daring and insolent men go there." If thru-hikers are to be thru-hikers, then cast their membership among the daring and insolent they must. Katahdin is there; it beckons; it is what they have come for.

It's only six miles to the top, and the first mile is easy enough. Soon, however, the Trail begins to curve up, straight up. Small rocks that lay on the Trail give way to larger ones that eventually give way to boulders. Hikers who look for the Trail to "even out" are in for a rude surprise. This Trail won't even out for another several miles. Instead it climbs up, up, relentlessly up, up amongst the trees, up beyond the blueberry bushes.

And still the Trail goes up, slowly up. The yellow birch trees shimmer gold in the sunlight and the early fallen leaves create a golden path beneath the hikers' boots. Hikers watch the boulders grow and they see the funny scoot marks on them, indicators of how hard it will be to come down. It isn't long before hiking becomes mountain climbing. If the tree leaves were a'flutter when the hiker started, then by the time the Trail crosses treeline, the wind simply roars, and a sense of peril rules. If the thru-hiker really wants to reach Baxter Peak, he or she must continue up. Sure, the views are unequaled as hikers look across evergreens that blanket the Maine woods. Sure, the ponds sparkle like blue diamonds as they adorn the landscape. But the hiker must continue to go up. Trees roots protruding from the earth, silken from the hands that have grasped them, provide rungs for hikers to pull themselves upward into the sky.

As the Trail continues its upward grind, hikers become one with the boulders, trying to find a purchase with either hand or boot, it doesn't matter which. Ordinary hikers, dizzy with vertigo, must stop. Ironically,

Six Pack and Shaggy after climbing Mt. Katahdin and finishing the AT.

this rocky world seems too unstable. Even as Wildhair climbed, and he was thrilled to climb with thru-hiker legend Bill Irwin, he "was never convinced" he would make it. The boulders that form the path have the power to change the simple hinge joint of the knee into a swivel, torn loose from its base.

"Having slumped, scrambled, rolled, bounced, and walked, by turns, over this scraggy country, I arrived . . . where rocks, gray, silent rocks, were the flocks and herds that pastured. They looked at me with hard gray eyes . . . It was a savage and dreary scenery enough . . . the mountain seemed a vast aggregation of loose rocks, as if some time it had rained rocks . . . I was deep within the hostile ranks of clouds . . . it reminded me of the creations of the old epic poets, of Atlas, Vulcan, the Cyclops, and Prometheus." So Thoreau described this wonderful and forbidding landscape. So the thru-hikers feel it also.

For some 2,158 miles, hiking the Appalachian Trail from Springer Mountain to Katahdin has been a rich tapestry of sensory experience. First it was a dream, then it was an idea. It became an obsession, a plan, a goal. It was by turns a project or an adventure, on other days a parade. It was a pain, a joy. It became an end unto itself, and then for the lucky hikers, a date. As the hikers climb together and reach out and touch the final white blaze together, as the thunder of their pulse dances with the roar of the wind, thru-hikers take their place in this most American of adventures.

a f t e r   t h e   t r a i l

Previous page: End of the Trail. Clockwise from front left: Crash, Lazylegs, Craig, Interplanet Janet, Pilgrim, Wildhair, and Just Harry.

I seem slowly to be adjusting back to 'normal' life. Somehow the AT seemed more exciting. It's odd to be clean, dry, and not smell bad— almost a novelty, really. People no longer stand 10 feet away when talking to me." — *Glider*

"I thoroughly enjoyed my experience on the mountains and in the Wilderness; it helps you see who you really are without all of the distractions of the busy, 'rat-race' world." — *Morning Glory*

"My six-week immersion into Trail life and performance under harsh conditions taught me more about myself than I could have ever imagined. I read once that the AT would do that for people, but it doesn't always reveal what the hiker hoped for . . . The part that most people I know don't get or can't understand is the mental atmosphere of the experience. With each step came a new thought . . . thoughts and how to get more of them. My whole operating system and values inventory were under self-scrutiny during those six and a half weeks. Every day's hike stripped away a little more of the layers of cultivated B.S." — *Kick-a-Tree*

"I don't know if it changed my life — I was pretty much on track to begin with — but it sure changed my perspective about what's important." — *Bloody Nose*

"The monotony is killing me. Every day for five months I saw something new. Although I can't face another mac-n-cheese, I just wish it never ended." — *Allgood*

"I watch the Weather Channel and think about the hikers still on the Trail and when I see tough weather, I remember places on the Trail and I think 'they gotta go through this? Yeesh.'" — *Wildhair*

"Life on the Trail is very simple . . . no pressures, few worries, and fewer responsibilities . . . it's like being a child all over again and having your summer vacation to play. Adjusting back to a life of responsibilities, cars, chaos, meetings, time-constraints, etc., is like growing up very quickly all over again and going from the naive innocence of a child to the hardened cold of an adult." — *Nomad*

"It was one of the most sustained physically demanding undertakings I have ever experienced and I congratulate all who are involved in making the AT truly one of the great mountain trails in the world." — *Kiwi*

"Out here, everyday is Saturday and every meal is a banquet. Back there, people just live for Friday." — *Lone Wolf*

"We have been off the Trail a few weeks now and have found no white blazes along city streets. People walking by generally avert their eyes and few offer a greeting. We have fallen into step with the off-Trail crowd and much too easily. A reason to be sad, perhaps, but also considering AT magic, a reason to go back." — *Download and Nexmo*

"Nothing can ever compare." — *Medusa*

"I changed after being gone two months . . . I appreciate things more. Like running water. Like hot water. Like any water. And food. There's lots of it, anytime. But I miss the Trail and everything about it . . . I know I'll be out there again. I don't know when and I don't know with whom. But I know once more I'll live the nomadic life I loved on the Appalachian Trail" — *Trail Gimp*

I have been given
One moment from heaven
As I am walking
Surrounded by night.
Stars high above me
Make a wish under moonlight.

On my way home
I remember
Only good days.
On my way home
I remember all the best days.
I'm on my way home,
I can remember
Every new day.

I move in silence
With each step taken,
Snow falling round me
Like angels in flight.
Far in the distance
Is my wish, under moonlight.

P.S. Would somebody pass the mac-n-cheese?

—- *Monkey Butt*

m a p s

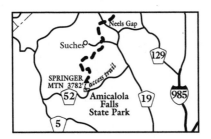

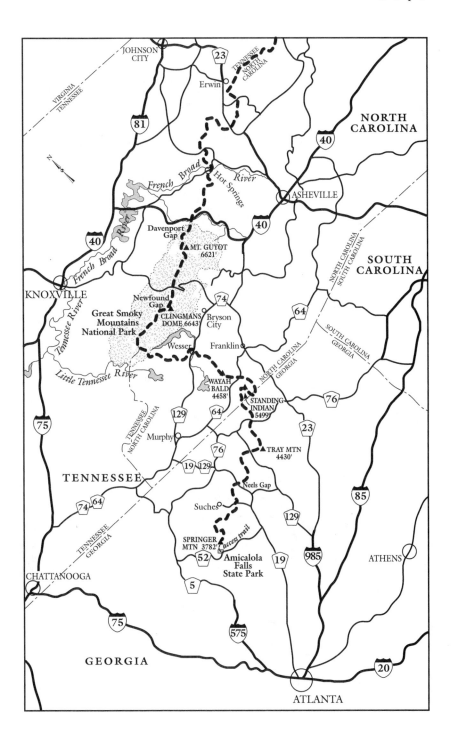

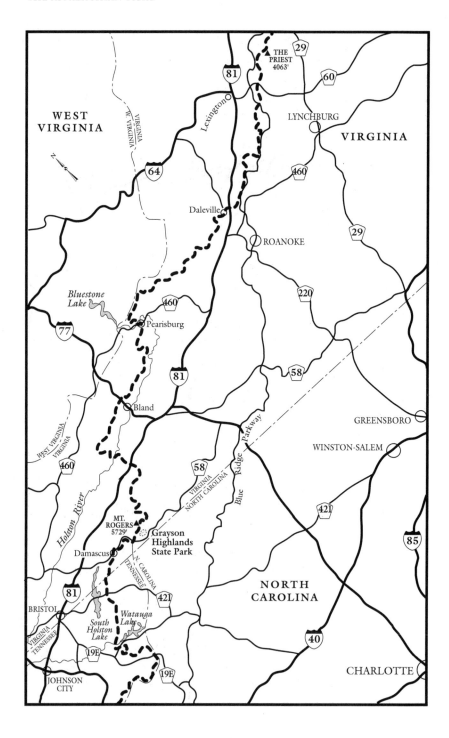

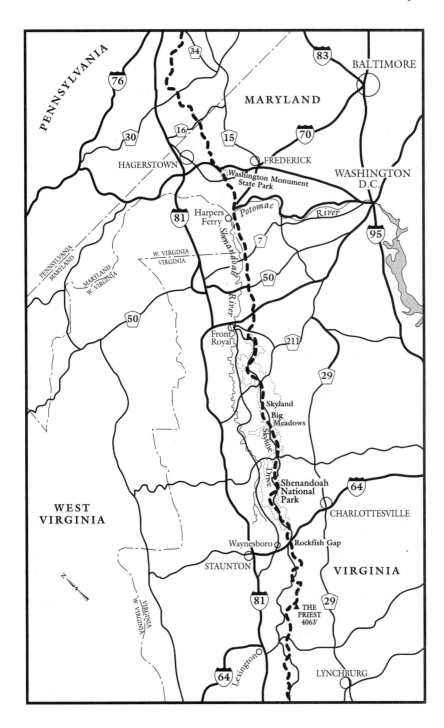

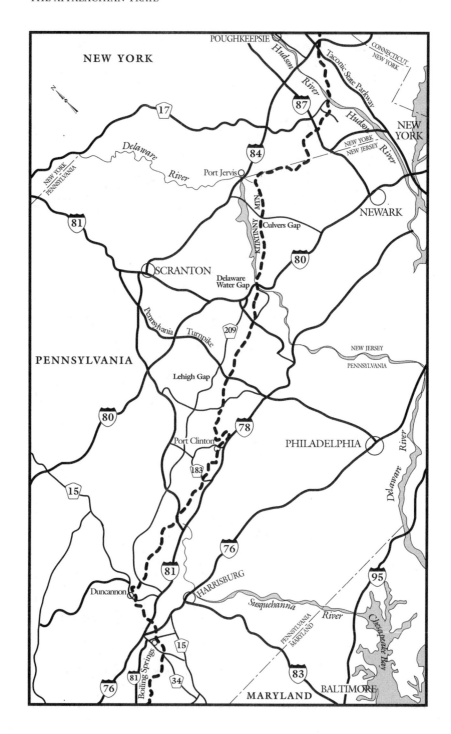

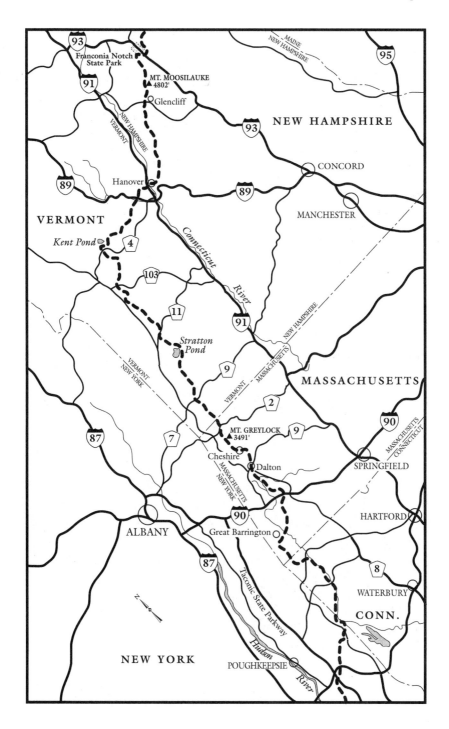

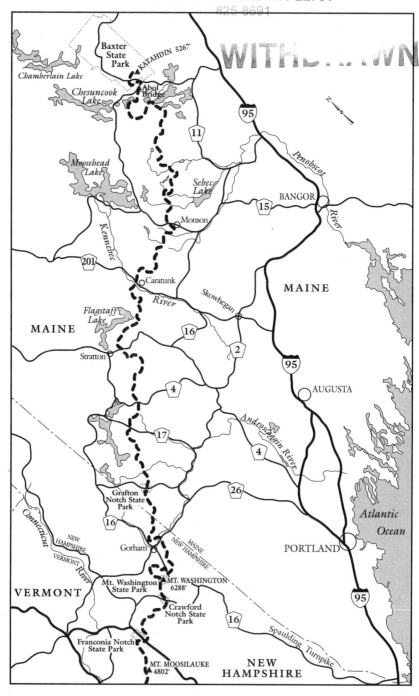